Readers of *Shakespeare for Everyone to Enjoy*
are saying. . . .

David Brown's enthusiasm for the works of Shakespeare is contagious!
We think Angus Bowmer would be pleased that his legacy at the
Oregon Shakespeare Festival continues to inspire playgoers of all ages.
Brown encourages those new to the theater experience to jump right in
as he shares ways to introduce students to these glorious plays.

William Patton   Shirley Patton

Executive Director 1953–1995   Actress 1955–1991

Oregon Shakespeare Festival

Having met the author, I can attest to his credibility in this subject.
Too often those who write about Shakespeare do not base their opinions on facts. This is a most enjoyable and factual read.

Dr. David Noebel

President and Founder of Summit Ministries, Manitou Springs, Colorado

The lover of Shakespeare will find much that will inspire him, but Professor Brown's offering is variously a theological reflection, a detailed
memoir of his unique experiences teaching and directing, and most
importantly—an impassioned invitation to the novice to come under
the spell of that greatest of dramatic conjurers.

Edward Hofmeister

Theatrical Professional, Graduate of University of Southern California

This is a book to be savored by both teachers and students. The author
communicates his extensive knowledge of the Bard's works with a
contagious enthusiasm that must surely win even those students who
have resisted getting to know the great playwright. In these pages it
becomes clear that Shakespeare is indeed for everyone to enjoy.

Mary-Elaine Swanson

Author of *The Education of James Madison*

This wonderful, little book is for those who love the Bard's plays but who are not Shakespeare scholars. I have loved Shakespeare for over 50 years, read all his plays, and have seen almost all his plays on stage, but have never, till I read David Brown's book, been introduced to the historical facts on Shakespeare's life, family, and work in an exciting and scholarly way for the average person. I will enthusiastically recommend this book to my friends, and we hope to go to Ashland this summer to get in on David Brown's lectures.

—Dr. Jay Grimstead
President and founder of Coalition on Revival, Murphys, California

During the last thirty-five years, the author has researched the Christian history of William Shakespeare and taught youth and adults how to discern the many Biblical analogies and presuppositions portrayed by his characters and themes. This volume can help you appreciate, as a good and profitable thing, the works of Shakespeare, "the Bard" or poet of the Bible.

—James B. Rose
President, American Christian History Institute

Shakespeare

for Everyone
to Enjoy

Shakespeare
for Everyone
to Enjoy

David R. Brown

An
Ascribed
Book

Imprint of **dg ink** Publishers

Daly City, California

Shakespeare for Everyone to Enjoy by David R. Brown

A Project of
The Noah Webster Educational Foundation

ISBN-10: 0-9772577-1-1
ISBN-13: 9780977257713
Library of Congress Control Number: 2007931140

An Ascribed Book

From *dg-ink* Publications
P.O. Box 1182
Daly City, CA 94015-1182
Contact: info@dg-ink.net
Website: www.dg-ink.net

Printed in the Canada

Cover and interior design by Desta Garrett

Cover painting: *Hamlet and the Grave Digger,* 1883 (oil on canvas)
    by Pascal Adolphe Jean Dagnan-Bouveret
    Courtesy of Julian Hartnoll, The Bridgeman Art Library
Grateful acknowledgment is made for permission to use:
Excerpt from the General Introduction (Section 2 "Records of the Life of Shakespeare") in *Shakespeare: Major Plays and the Sonnets* by G. B. Harrison, copyright 1948 by Harcourt, Inc. and renewed 1975 by G. B. Harrison; reprinted by permission of the publisher.

Dedication

In Memoriam

DR. FRANK BAXTER
Professor Emeritus
English Literature & Shakespeare Studies
The University of Southern California
Los Angeles, California

DR. ANGUS L. BOWMER
Founder
The Oregon Shakespeare Festival
Ashland, Oregon

Contents

William

Shakespeare

Foreword

*A*FTER many years of teaching Shakespeare at the college and high school levels, my associates suggested that I ought to write a book detailing some of my lectures. In addition, I was challenged to relate my experiences while directing three of his plays. As I pondered over my notes and reflected on my work, I concluded that too many people do not enjoy Shakespeare. My experience has been that the more I studied these great plays, the more I developed a love for the works of the greatest playwright in history.

My primary objective in writing this book is to open up new vistas to Shakespeare's plays. As I struggled to decide how I could best relate my own pilgrimage, I began to sense a deep desire to help those who have little or no experience in studying Shakespeare or in attending live performances of his plays. Also, I wrestled over what would be the best way to try to dispel the negative reactions that so many have expressed to me after attending a play or viewing a video or movie.

A second objective is to provide homeschools and Christian schools a means for studying Shakespeare, especially in independent study groups. During the time that I served as the superintendent of Christian Heritage Academy, we added an independent study section to our school. The parents whose children were enrolled in this section told me that they could not find any suitable material to help their children with a study of Shakespeare's works. Hopefully this book will help to fill that need. However, this book has been written to challenge all students to delve into a richer understanding of his plays and sonnets.

First of all, the student must rid himself of any previous thoughts or ideas that might hinder his quest to develop an interest in studying Shakespeare. Negative views about the Bard and his plays must be cast aside. Without an open mind, the student will often miss the gems of wisdom waiting to be discovered. No matter how many times I have studied, lectured on, or attended live performances of Shakespeare's plays, I always discover something I had previously missed. A strong, positive attitude will serve you well when you start your adventure into the wonderful world of Shakespeare.

Secondly, one who values the truth will put aside all attempts to read into Shakespeare's plays conceptual material that he never intended to write. Today it is in vogue for a director to put his own value system and message into his production of the play, so that Shakespeare's original intent is lost. This destroys the enjoyment of the play. The life and work of the Bard of Avon is often viewed from conjecture and mere guesswork. Our desire is to look at the facts, many of which can be documented. This book includes in the appendix a listing of most of the indisputable records. The appendix also contains the last will and testament of William Shakespeare.

Finally, I want to encourage the reader to commit himself to a deeper study of what was once considered an indispensable subject in an academic curriculum in American education. When I attended high school, a class including at least one Shakespeare play was a requirement for graduation. Most colleges and universities offered Shakespeare courses, which were required for an English literature major. Too often in recent times, instead of teaching the works of Shakespeare, the writings of authors whose works cannot match the power and beauty of England's finest playwright are being substituted.

Special thanks to Alice Eller, who has spent countless hours editing this book, and to Beth Ballenger, Founder and Director of the Noah Webster Educational Foundation, for encouraging the production of this book, Linda Jay Geldens, Adam Brink, and Mary-Elaine Swanson for proofreading the text, to Desta Garrett of *dg ink* for design, layout, and publishing, and to Helen Cook, publicist. I am also grateful to my wife and three sons, who attended many of my lectures, and to my sons for their participation in the plays I directed at American Heritage Christian High School. My thanks to all my students, whose encouragement has contributed to making this book a reality.

David R. Brown
Newark, California
2007

Chapter One

"O for a Muse of Fire"
Introduction

O for a Muse of fire, that would ascend
The brightest heaven of invention,
A kingdom for a stage, princes to act
And monarchs to behold the swelling scene!

CHORUS, Prologue to *King Henry the Fifth*

MANY people today think that the plays of William Shakespeare are boring, too difficult to understand, or simply not relevant for our time. Some may object to the language. Others say his plays are too sophisticated. Then there are those people who, after attending one bad performance of a Shakespearean play, decided they would not enjoy any of Shakespeare's plays. Because of this, they refuse to attend any more productions written by the greatest playwright of all times.

What these people have failed to realize is that Shakespeare wrote for the purpose of bringing entertainment to the stage for men, women, and children of diverse classes and backgrounds to enjoy. This is one of the reasons scholars and patrons call him a genius. He instinctively knew how to reach every audience and what to write so they would leave the theater with a desire to come back again.

In all his plays, Shakespeare had one primary motive: to entertain. Many playwrights do not follow this principle. They choose to write plays that appeal to what is politically correct or put forth a moral agenda. If the primary objective of a play is something other than entertainment, the play will only appeal to a limited audience and fail to bring in a broad base of patrons.

Because Shakespeare understood good business principles, he was prepared to compete at the highest level of theater, the London stage. He may have learned this while growing up in Stratford, helping his father in his successful business as a tanner and seller of leather goods. He would have had ample opportunity to observe the things that caused problems in the growth of the leather shop. If the shop did not make money, the family was in trouble.

As a boy, one of the great advantages for Will was the character of his parents. It does make a difference for a boy to live in a home where the parents exhibit strong Christian faith and convictions. This will be documented in the chapter on the life of William Shakespeare. Honesty, frugality, perseverance, and other character traits would have been encouraged. The records indicate that his father, John Shakespeare, was probably a strict but loving disciplinarian.

At some point, Will became aware of the theater. Will would have had ample opportunity to observe the theater in Stratford, as traveling troupes performed there occasionally. It is possible, although we have no specific record, that his parents may have taken him to one of the famous stages of London. Somewhere in his personal experience with theater and business, Will learned the importance of this one great purpose of all theater: audiences must be entertained!

Since Elizabethan audiences found great enjoyment even at his first play, Shakespeare was quickly established as the leading playwright in London.[1] This success continued throughout his career, with even greater attendance and longer runs of his later plays. The popularity of his plays did not end with his career. However, he probably never imagined that four hundred years later, audiences would still be attending his plays and studying them as literature.

Why then do so many people say that they do not enjoy Shakespeare, or that they are not interested? There are several problems that have arisen in today's culture. First of all, our education system has slowly dropped its emphasis upon classical education. In fact, most public schools have dropped Shakespeare along with Latin and other classical studies from their curricula. Closely related to this is the failure to develop an extensive vocabulary. Scholarship does not appeal to lazy minds. That is why many people will not even attempt to read Shakespeare or the King James Bible.

Another roadblock to the enjoyment of Shakespeare is the failure to produce his plays as he wrote them. That was one of the principles I learned from Angus Bowmer, the founder of the Oregon Shakespeare Festival. He said one of his main desires in producing the plays was to attempt to reproduce the plays the way Shakespeare originally intended. This, of course, is a matter of interpretation. When the interpretation is based on an intense study of the original material, it is more likely to result in a production that comes close to the author's intent. I was thrilled one summer when attending a superb production of *King Richard the Second* at Ashland, Oregon, to hear the woman next to me exclaim: "Now that's the way I enjoy a Shakespeare play, when it is performed the way Shakespeare did it."

When the audience is distracted by bizarre "gimcracks,"[2] improper dress (or various degrees of undress), it is extremely difficult to follow the plot line. Sometimes even putting the actors in common street clothes can be a distraction because many audiences are expecting Elizabethan or other appropriate period costumes. If the distractions are overwhelming, many playgoers will lose interest or become so irate that they cannot enjoy the production. However, it is possible to produce Shakespeare in modern clothing without losing continuity or the audience's attention when the director carefully blends the Elizabethan language and setting with a contemporary atmosphere that appears normal to those watching the performance.

One more common failure in our contemporary American drama scene is the desire to read into a Shakespearean play some cultural or political agenda that simply is not in the lines of the play, or if hinted at in the lines, was not intended by Shakespeare to be a dominant theme. Many years ago, we attended a production of *Timon of Athens* in the Bowmer Theatre. The setting for the play was a military insurgence in

Latin America, with both men and women soldiers. In the courtyard following the play, we met Dr. Bowmer who was then retired from the position of artistic director at the Oregon Shakespeare Theater. He asked me what I thought about the play, and I responded that I left the theater totally confused. Then he replied: "I talked to the director about this and he showed me the lines. Yes, these minor points are in the lines, but they should not dominate the setting or the plot. Unfortunately, this is what we have to look forward to in experimental theater!"

In some cases, a director will overemphasize the description of a minor character (or characters) to the point that the actors distract the audience from following the main plot and theme of the play. In other presentations, I have left the play feeling that the director had intended to leave the audience with the thought that immoral behavior is desirable. The truth of the matter is that Shakespeare always treats bad behavior as tragic or puts it into a comic situation where a member of the audience might identify with the condition and learn to laugh at himself for his own failures.

In fact, many teachers who have spent years delving into the depths of Shakespeare's plays have concluded that infidelity brings disaster. From this perspective, Shakespeare differs noticeably from his contemporaries and many of the dramatists of the Restoration and of modern Broadway. A noted scholar, G. B. Harrison, states: "He has plenty of jokes about cuckolds' horns, as have all Elizabethan dramatists, but he sees nothing comic in unfaithfulness or unchastity, which always bring disaster."[3]

A deep enthusiasm for the works of Shakespeare is acquired through a long process. Probably the most important factor for me has been the association with others who have passed on to me the satisfaction they have derived from both reading the plays and seeing good productions. Two of my teachers at East High in Denver inspired me by giving our class an opportunity to experience a taste of his plays. First, my tenth-grade literature teacher led us through a study of *Julius Caesar.* The following year, I was fortunate to have a speech teacher who used famous lines from a variety of Shakespeare's plays to teach us how to emphasize certain techniques in public speaking.

Later, when I was attending the University of Southern California, I signed up for a two-unit literature course which included a study of *Hamlet*. This professor noticed how enthusiastic I was during this study. He called me aside one day, and said: "We have the best Shakespeare professor in America right here at USC, Dr. Frank Baxter." The next semester, I signed up for Dr. Baxter's Shakespeare class. I was not disappointed.

There were no assigned seats in Frank Baxter's classes. The front seats were taken by those students lucky enough to have classes in Founders Hall the previous hour. I was one of those who had to cross the entire campus, so I regularly sat in the back row of the auditorium. This did not deter my interest. I literally hung on every word as Dr. Baxter took us through about half of the canon, including all of Shakespeare's most popular plays.

Many years later, when I was a pastor in Medford, Oregon, Bill and Shirley Patton (members of our church) introduced me to Angus Bowmer. While I had gained an academic appreciation for Shakespeare the man and the power of his dramatic writings from Dr. Baxter, I learned the methodology for staging a Shakespearean play from Dr. Bowmer. Years later, while I was teaching Shakespeare classes at American Heritage Christian High School in Hayward, I was able to use this invaluable training to direct three Shakespearean plays using high school students in both cast and production.

The secret to the enjoyment of Shakespeare is often found with those who have gained an understanding of and devotion to the greatest playwright in history. It is the purpose of this book to open up that secret to you, the readers, so that you may come to the same love and appreciation of this great literature.

---

1 This can be documented by the receipts at the box office, showing his first play taking in receipts far above average. "Records in the Life of Shakespeare," 1592, March 3, in G. B. Harrison, ed., *Shakespeare, Major Plays*, N.Y.: Harcourt Brace, 1948, 9. (Appendix I, 109–119.)

2 *gimcracks:* A trivial mechanism; a device; a toy; a pretty thing. Noah Webster. *An American Dictionary of the English Language* (Facsimile 1828 edition). San Francisco: Foundation for American Christian Education, 1967.

3 Harrison, 1948, 6. (Appendix I, 109–119.)

Chapter Two

"This Happy Breed of Men"
The Universality of Shakespeare

This earth of majesty, this seat of Mars,
This other Eden, demi-Paradise,
This fortress built by Nature for herself
Against infection and the hand of war,
This happy breed of men. . . .

John of Gaunt, *King Richard the Second*, ACT II, SCENE 1

ILLIAM SHAKESPEARE is one of the greatest English writers of all time. Although there are many varied reasons for his incredible success as a dramatist, his unique understanding of human character was of primary importance. From this ability to reach into the depths of character development came his special appeal to all types of people. On the Elizabethan stage there was a fierce competition for a universal audience. Although there were many other good writers in his day, from his very first play it was evident that Shakespeare had an ability to reach a large, diverse audience.

The Bard of Stratford was just as comfortable speaking to the "ground-lings"[1] as he was speaking to royalty. He had developed empathy toward the common man, and he was equally concerned over the plight of men in higher stations of life. No other playwright from the Elizabethan period displays such a depth of commitment to reach all levels of society.

Although Shakespeare was an Englishman in every sense of the term, he showed a great concern for those of other nationalities. For example, even the hated French were given a degree of respect in his plays. He especially romanticized the Italians; but he also wrote much about the

Greeks, the Trojans, the Romans, the Egyptians, and the Danes. A study of his thirty-seven plays reveals a broad scope of backgrounds used in the development of each of his characters. Even characters in minor roles were often given special treatment so that the audience could easily identify with a person of lesser importance.

In reading Shakespeare's plays, we become aware of his interest in people from all walks of life. Although he was a Christian, he did not leave Jews, agnostics, and those of other religions represented in London at that time out of his plays. He seemed just as much at home with those whose opinions differed from his own as with those who strongly agreed with him. Because of this wide focus on all aspects of life, he attracted to his plays a wider audience than most of his contemporary writers.

Furthermore, he chose all types to serve in the roles of both tragic and comic circumstances. Shylock, the Jew in *The Merchant of Venice*, is a good example of both a tragic figure and one that is also somewhat comic. In *Twelfth Night*, Malvolio, who is a Puritan, demonstrates both tragic and comic elements. Falstaff, who once was a respected knight as well as a college student, shows both the comic and tragic elements in his fall from a high station in life to one who carouses with low-life people. Shakespeare created Falstaff as a comic character in his plays, *Henry IV*, Parts 1 and 2. The comic Falstaff was so popular with the Elizabethan audiences that Shakespeare was encouraged to write a play in which Falstaff would be the central comic figure: *The Merry Wives of Windsor*.

The tragic nature of Falstaff is described in *Henry V*. We learn that Falstaff had become a victim of false expectations. Because he had developed a close friendship with his buddy (then Prince Hal), he assumed that a great future awaited him when Hal was crowned as Henry V. He imagined that the new king would appoint him to some high political office. However, Shakespeare's picture of Henry V is that of a great king, who would have no place in his government for a loser like Falstaff.

Shakespeare is very familiar with the daily plight of prostitutes and thieves, but he is just as familiar with those in the royal court. Some have suggested that he had to have experienced all these various degrees of

Shakespeare for Everyone to Enjoy

social life in order to write so precisely about them. Others have thought that he must have traveled to Italy, Greece, and other countries in order to learn so many precise details about different types of nationalities and peoples. However, it is my belief, since we have no records that he ever attended a university or had any higher education, that in his early years he became an avid reader who developed an intense interest in all types of characters and foreign places. The facts would also indicate that he lived most of his life in the town of Stratford-on-Avon. At some point in his twenties he went to London to begin his vocation on the stage. These facts will be documented in the next chapter.

It should also be noted that the plays of Shakespeare are divided (by scholars) into three general types: comedies, tragedies, and histories. His deep understanding of history was revealed as he began to write historical plays, in which his audience could identify with the great figures of English history. His primary source for English history was Raphael Holinshed's *Chronicles of England, Scotland, and Ireland*, published in 1577 and reissued in a second edition in 1587.[2]

This quality in the art of drama has been called universality.[3] Harrison believes that the one quality that contributes most to Shakespeare's universality is wisdom; that is, his ability to understand and sympathize more than other men. Harrison further describes this universal quality in the works of Shakespeare by emphasizing his ability to see human character in the whole picture so that people from every country, creed, and generation grasp the power and imagery found in a Shakespearean play.[4]

It is also clear, in looking at the success of Shakespeare's plays when performed on the Elizabethan stage, that he drew audiences from all walks of life. The box office receipts alone attest to his ability to draw large and diverse audiences.[5] The major reason for this was that Shakespeare wrote his plays for everyone.

When Shakespeare's plays are performed by companies whose goal is to produce his plays in the appropriate manner, audiences of diverse backgrounds attend regularly. That is why we attend the Oregon Shakespeare Festival in Ashland each summer. Since 1969, we have taken a group of

Shakespeare enthusiasts to see the plays and discuss the details, often relating themes and characters to Biblical principles.

In 1969, some church leaders in our summer camping program proposed that we offer a conference to families from the various churches of Southern Oregon, using the plays in Ashland as a focal point. I was asked to be the director of this Shakespeare camp. The best person to be the lecturer, I thought, would be Dr. Frank Baxter, then Professor Emeritus at the University of Southern California. When I called Dr. Baxter on the phone, he replied, "I'm 75 years old, and I'm just not able to do this any more." My next question to Dr. Baxter was, "Whom would you suggest to lead this conference?" His answer was a major shock. "What about you? Do you still have my notes? There is no one for whom I could give a higher recommendation!"

I was in such a state of shock that I wanted to run away from the whole project. I had never lectured on Shakespeare before, nor had I any experience in teaching his plays. I settled on inviting a professor of English literature from the University of Oregon at Eugene to be our lecturer. The conference was a great success. Each day he would give us the background material for each play. In the evening the group would attend the play, and the next morning we would talk about Scriptural principles and values that we observed. But the story does not end there.

In the fall of that same year, our family moved to Newark, California, where I served as senior pastor of the First Presbyterian Church. A local organization that coordinated summer youth programs for the local churches asked me to attend a meeting for the planning of the summer activities. Several young people spoke about camps and seminars that they had attended the previous summer. The chairman asked me what types of activities I had planned while I was in Oregon. At this point I related to the group my experience with the Shakespeare family camp in the Ashland area.

Immediately after I had finished describing our camp, several young people expressed a strong desire to have a Shakespeare conference for young people. There was so much enthusiasm that I decided to direct the group and attempt the lectures on the plays. The Shakespeare conference was billed as the premier event for Christian youth in the summer brochure for the 1970 youth program. I contacted the Presbyterian Church in Ashland, and my long-time friend, Rev. B. J. Holland, pastor, invited us to stay in his fellowship hall and adjoining house without charge.

Thirty high-school age youths signed up, and we enlisted the aid of three other adults. The indoor Bowmer Theatre had opened that spring, which allowed us to see four (three outdoor plus one indoor) Shakespeare plays. The young people took turns in the cooking of the meals and cleaning up afterwards. I followed the same format we had used the previous summer, and I was amazed by the intelligent responses expressed by these young people. How quickly they picked out the religious themes and spiritual values! In fact, they were much sharper in their responses than some of the adults at the conference of the previous year. The amazing thing about this first summer youth Shakespeare conference was the price: $33.00 per student, which included travel costs, all four tickets, food, insurance, and the cost to bring four adults, who were not required to pay. And we ended up the trip with a slight profit!

A tradition had begun. The following year we offered the program again, and twenty-four students came. As the years continued to pass, every summer my family offered to assist me with the Ashland conference. Although we had a number of young people who returned on a regular basis, very rarely did any of the new students have an understanding of the works of William Shakespeare. Often we would have a student who had never read or seen a Shakespearean play. These students came from a great variety of backgrounds, most of them attending on the recommendation of those who had previously been to Ashland.

Children under the age of five are not allowed to attend the plays. During our first conferences, we had to secure a sitter for our children. As my sons reached their fifth birthday, they could not wait to join us at the plays and lectures. After ten years of youth conferences in Ashland, the First Presbyterian Church sold the hall and the attached house to a local service club.

At this point we decided to hold our conference at the Glenyan Campgrounds, just a few miles east of Ashland, on the road to Klamath Falls. The program began moving from a youth program to a family camp. Now some of our older students stay in a local motel, but the lectures are held at camp. Several times, I have considered discontinuing this annual event. However, it has now become such an integral part of family life that it would not seem like summer if we did not make the trek to Ashland. My sons attend whenever their schedules permit them to be free, which is almost every year. My middle son, Mark, brings his wife and children regularly. Mark's family stayed at a motel the first year they had children, but they have decided that they prefer camping. A few families bring motor homes to the campground; but most like the tent sites, where we can look up at the stars at night. Some families even bring telescopes. We have concluded that we like the mixture of the Oregon countryside and the experience of attending marvelous plays.

After several years of lecturing in the summer conferences at Ashland, I began teaching at Chabot College in Hayward, California. Most of my classes were based on subjects from the Bible or directly related to Biblical subjects and church history. I began to weave into some of my classes appropriate sections from the plays of Shakespeare. After a couple of years, I developed a course that I entitled "Shakespeare and the Bible." Most of the students responded positively to my new focus, and a few even attended our Shakespeare conference.

In the meantime, my wife began teaching elementary classes at a Christian school, also in Hayward. After she had been on the faculty for three years, she told me there was an opening in the high school for an English literature teacher. I applied for the job and was accepted. The second year, I offered a class on Shakespeare to members of the junior and senior classes. Some of these students, as well as a few members of the faculty, attended our summer program in Ashland.

Throughout my entire teaching career, I have never yet found a student who, after a time of studying the works of the master, told me that he did not like Shakespeare's plays. This fact impresses on me the reality of the universality of Shakespeare. The bard of Stratford truly wrote his plays for everyone.

---

1 *groundling*: one who paid the lowest price for a theater ticket and stood (or sat) on the ground, open air, section of the audience.

2 Harrison, *Shakespeare, Major Plays*, 103.

3 Ibid., 3.

4 Ibid.

5 Ibid., 5. (Note: For the 15 performances of *Henry VI*, the gross takings were 32£, 8 shillings or an average of 2£, 3 shillings a performance. The average for all other plays in London over 4 months' time was 1£, 14 shillings a performance.)

Chapter Three

"*This Was a Man!*"
The Life of Shakespeare

His life was gentle, and the elements
So mixed in him that Nature might stand up
And say to all the world, 'This was a man!'

Julius Caesar, ACT V, SCENE 5

THE biographical material on William Shakespeare has been limited to those actual facts that can be documented. In studying the life of Shakespeare, it is important for the scholar to know where fact ends and where guessing begins. These records, which have been indisputably authenticated, are considerable.[1] In and of themselves, they should dispel any doubt about whether he was a real, historical person, or whether some other person wrote his plays.

In Elizabethan times, family records were kept in the local parish church; therefore, we do not know the actual birth date of William Shakespeare. However, the date of his baptism has been recorded as April 26, 1564.[2] The custom was to baptize a child as soon after his birth as possible. Thus, there is no strong reason to reject the traditional date for his birth, April 23. His father, John Shakespeare, had come to Stratford-on-Avon in the 1550s and had become a successful businessman. The records show that John was a landowner and that he had a thriving business in leather goods. In 1564 he was elected to the office of alderman, and in 1568 to bailiff, the highest office in the town (a role equivalent to our mayor). Although we have no records to support Will's early education, men of John Shakespeare's position in the community would have sent their sons to the local grammar school.

The free school at Stratford was financed by the Guild of the Holy Cross, and the charter stipulated that the town was to have a "free grammar school for the training and education of children to be continued forever."[3] William Shakespeare would have learned how to read and write before entering the school. Since the schoolboys were required to learn these basics before entering grammar school, Will probably learned them from the parish clerk, or from his mother at home.

The curriculum, as in most other schools in England during the Elizabethan period, was very serious, thorough, and quite dull. These schools were formed after the medieval pattern; thus, Latin was the primary subject. The text used was William Lily's Latin grammar. Occasionally, there was a teacher in the school who helped the students over the tedious rules with its exact verb and noun forms so that the student could concentrate on reading Latin literature. Shakespeare may have had such a teacher. First, the accomplished Latin student would have studied Julius Caesar's *Gallic Wars;* then came Cicero, whose speeches taught the Latin student much about the Republic of Rome and its eventual demise. The student would go on to study Virgil and Ovid, both poets. It should be noted that most of the mythology in Shakespeare's plays was based on what he had learned from Ovid's *Metamorphoses.*[4]

There was also an emphasis on speaking Latin publicly. This would have introduced William to the importance of good elocution, also needed by good actors. In fact, many schoolmasters allowed their students to act out Latin plays by Plautus and Terence, which would have given them even more practice in the art of public speaking. A good teacher would require his boys to develop a controlled and intelligent use of the voice. If William had had such a teacher, we can see how that teacher might have provided him with some inspiration toward acting and writing plays. However, no single schoolmaster was given the privilege of tutoring young Shakespeare. The records from Stratford show that there were three schoolmasters during the time William would have been at the grammar school. They were Walter Roche, Simon Hunt, and Thomas Jenkins, all of whom were university graduates of Oxford, presumably

Shakespeare for Everyone to Enjoy

competent and well-trained. Since there are no records to establish fact, we can only guess that each man had some small part in the education of the boy who would become the world's greatest playwright.[5] It should also be noted that the average day for boys in the grammar school was long, often beginning at seven in the morning and ending at five in the evening, with two hours off for dinner. This would allow very little time for leisure activities, but also demonstrates why very few Elizabethan schoolboys ever got involved in criminal activity.

During those times the family business usually involved every member of the family, and often the oldest son was expected to carry on the business after the father died. At some point, probably between the beginning of the seventh and ending of his eighth grade, his father, John Shakespeare, may have begun to suffer financial losses. Therefore, William may have been needed to help in the leather business full-time. Although this cannot be verified, there is no evidence that William had any formal education beyond grammar school.

Another gap in the records of the life of William Shakespeare is between his early days in Stratford and his involvement in the theatrical world of London. We can only speculate concerning his motivations and early desires. Whatever the case, there were many opportunities for young Will to see public entertainments. No fair would have been complete without various types of entertainers. Among these were actors who put on short plays or skits. But Stratford also had real productions, staged by touring companies, which appeared regularly in the more prosperous towns. An Act of Parliament rigidly licensed these companies because of problems that arose when groups of men began going about the country without proper credentials. Also, the tour company had to enlist the approval of the town officials. Since William was the son of one of the most prominent men of the Council, he may have had opportunities to see some of these plays in preview. Most of the plays by these groups at the time of his childhood were morality plays, whose moral principles and lessons would have had the approval of parents who wanted their sons and daughters to admire Christian character.[6]

The next official record in the life of William Shakespeare was his marriage, at the age of 18, to Anne Hathaway on November 28, 1582. Anne was eight years older than her husband; however, in a small community, the two families probably would have had a close relationship. Much has been made of the hasty marriage, but even that was not entirely unusual according to marriage customs at that time. Richard Hathaway, Anne's father, died a year before her marriage, but he had left her a marriage portion in his will. John Shakespeare and Richard Hathaway may have agreed to the marriage before the death of Anne's father. Both families were solid families in Stratford, and the custom in those days was that the fathers usually allowed their children to court before marriage, and then to enter into a pre-marriage contract. Furthermore, the record shows that a pre-marriage contract had been signed long before the actual marriage. In addition, William and Anne had the blessing of the Bishop of Worcester to solemnize the marriage with the asking of the banns only once.[7]

On May 26, 1583, the first child, Susanna, daughter of William Shakespeare was baptized. Then on February 2, 1585, the parish register recorded the birth of twins: Hamnet and Judith, to William Shakespeare. It would appear that during this time William worked in his father's business in Stratford. However, we have no records to verify this; it is only conjecture.

In fact, the next recorded facts are from March 3, 1592, nine years later. Henslowe, whose diary lists payments to many dramatists of that day, records the great financial success from a play, *Harry the Sixth*.[8] It is very likely that this referred to William Shakespeare's play, *Henry VI, Part One*. What we must conclude is that Shakespeare had then embarked upon a career with an acting company in London. There is absolutely no factual evidence telling us why and when he left Stratford to go to London for a vocation on the stage. It would seem likely that he came to London before 1592. Since acting companies were usually composed of a group of men who shared multiple roles in a company until they had established themselves as actors or playwrights, William Shakespeare probably would have joined one of these established companies in 1590 or 1591. On September 3, 1592, Robert Greene's papers referred to an "upstart

Crow . . . the only Shake-scene in a country."[9] If Shakespeare had been writing plays for several years, Greene would not have referred to him as an "upstart." Therefore, he most likely began to write plays in 1591 or 1592.

On April 18, 1593, a Stratford man by the name of Richard Field entered at Stationers' Register a lengthy poem entitled *Venus and Adonis* by William Shakespeare. (This could imply that William had already established a reputation for writing poetry in Stratford.) On May 9, 1594, another poem by Shakespeare, *The Rape of Lucrece*, was entered for printing. Both of these poems were dedicated to the Earl of Southampton. The frequency of references complimentary to these poems, along with the large number of editions issued, was proof that Shakespeare had established himself as a poet of note.[10]

On December 26 and 27, 1594, the account of the Treasurer of the Chamber recorded that payment was made to William Kempe, Richard Burbage, and William Shakespeare, members of the Lord Chamberlain's Company, for their performance of two comedies before the Queen at Greenwich Palace.[11] The important thing to note here is that this is the first record that Shakespeare was a member of this important acting company. We have no record that he had joined any other company before this time, but it could be inferred. There have been many conjectures about his work in London before he was established, in this case as an actor. We do know that he had done some acting before or during his writing. Several theories have been put forth concerning his previous work. Since many playwrights in those days worked on plays together, there is some thought that he may have collaborated with other playwrights, such as Christopher Marlowe, until he had established himself as a writer.

Unfortunately, we have no records about his family that would establish the location of the family residence during Shakespeare's early days in London. Did his wife and children remain at Stratford? Or did they move with him to London after he had become established? Was Shakespeare a commuter between Stratford and London? (The time to go from Stratford to London has been estimated as a three-day trip.) Since most of the plays were in the open air, the play season ran from May to October. Certainly, after he had become a famous playwright (about 1596), he could have done more of his writing in Stratford. The facts are of some help: on May 4, 1597, William Shakespeare purchased New Place, the largest home in Stratford, from William Underhill for sixty pounds sterling. Although we cannot supply the information for previous years, it is clear that Shakespeare and his family had their primary residence in Stratford from that point on.

In 1596, tragedy struck the Shakespeare home. On August 11, the parish register of the Stratford-on-Avon church records the burial of William Shakespeare's only son, Hamnet.[12] Most scholars believe that Shakespeare may have been away from Stratford at the time of his son's death. There are no records to establish the cause of Hamnet's death or whether his father was out of town at the time of his passing. The death of his only son would have been a major setback for the playwright, especially if he had been away from home when his son died. It is my personal belief that the Shakespeare family was strong and united, and that they would have supported each other in this time of grief.

William had always shown great respect for his father and mother. It is most likely that he likewise showed concern for the care of his wife and children. Although his business was in London, he was drawn as much as possible to the town of his roots. It was the year following the death of Hamnet when William Shakespeare purchased New Place.[13] Since London was not the kind of city where a man of Shakespeare's character would have wanted to raise his family, Stratford would have been the logical place to ensure that his wife and children would have the best life. It was also the home of both Will and Anne's parents. With the purchase of a large home, he would also have a quiet place where he could write while away from London. His business in the city was well established after becoming a key factor in the success of Lord Chamberlain's Men. It also seems reasonable to assume that after 1597, Shakespeare traveled frequently between London and Stratford.

On October 20, 1596, John Shakespeare was granted by the College of Heralds a coat of arms, which entitled both John and William the right to be called "gentlemen." It is reasonable to assume that since William had achieved great success in the theater, he would have had some influence in attaining this honor for his family. The coat of arms gave to an entire family a special place in Elizabethan society. These arms may now be seen on the monument over William Shakespeare's grave, which was placed in a prominent setting in Stratford's Trinity Church.[14]

Beginning in 1598, the records show that William Shakespeare was writing and producing several plays a year. The Lord Chamberlain's Men had become *the* major acting company in London. On February 21, 1599, a lease for the land on which the Globe Theatre would eventually be built was agreed between Nicholas Brend and several members of Shakespeare's company. Of particular note is the inclusion of Cuthbert and Richard Burbage. Richard was the leading actor in the company, and both he and his brother had spent many years on the stage since they were the sons of James Burbage, who had built one of the finest theaters of the day, simply called The Theatre. In fact, to James this theater was "the one important structure in England."[15]

On September 8, 1601, John Shakespeare was buried, according to the parish records. John left to his son, William, the two houses on Henley Street. William's mother, Mary (Arden), lived in one of them until her death in 1608. William paid a grand tribute to his mother when he wrote his great comedy, *As You Like It*. In this play, most of the action takes place in the Forest of Arden. On May 1, 1602, William Shakespeare bought a piece of property in old Stratford from William and John Combe. The deed was then delivered to Gilbert Shakespeare, William's younger brother.[16] These facts give strong evidence that William Shakespeare was a man who loved his entire family dearly.

In 1594, Shakespeare, who by this time was writing as many as five plays a year, had unquestionably become a noted playwright. Many records detail when his plays were produced as well as their financial success. Altogether, he produced thirty-seven plays, and possibly collaborated with other writers on several more. Shakespeare may have also written plays for which we have no record. The play writing dates parallel the purchase of New Place and tend to corroborate my theory that he did most of his writing at Stratford. His plays are often grouped in three time periods: 1591–1594, his early plays; from 1595 to 1605, his middle plays, which in my opinion include his greatest works; and the years 1606–1613 for his last and more involved plays.[17]

The Globe Theatre was built by Shakespeare's company in 1599. It was octagonal in shape and built near the Rose Theatre on the south bank of the Thames River. Most of the theaters were erected on that side of the Thames, across the river from the main part of London. The theaters were all public, open air, made of wood, but outside the city limits; therefore, they were free from the jurisdiction of London officials. After the Globe burned, a new Globe was erected on the same spot in 1613. Several other theaters had been built nearby when the second Globe was completed.[18] In the 1590s James Burbage bought the old Blackfriars monastery, hoping to remodel it as an indoor theater. It was also in a fashionable residential area, and he thought he could charge much higher ticket prices than were paid in the public outdoor theaters. However, the residents of the area complained to the city officials that this indoor theater would be a nuisance, and the Privy Council ordered Burbage not to open the Blackfriars Theatre. Soon afterwards, James Burbage died. In 1608 Shakespeare's company acquired the use of the Blackfriars, a private theater, and began producing plays by candlelight. This began to attract a more sophisticated audience to these indoor plays, and the theater tended to be less public, reaching a better class of patronage.[19]

Queen Elizabeth died on March 24, 1603. When King James ascended the throne, he changed the Lord Chamberlain's Men to the King's Men. The company was now directly sponsored by the King of England. From Shakespeare and his fellow actors' point of view, what had first concerned them was the king's personal opinions about the theater. There had been considerable apprehension among the members of the King's Men that King James might attempt to exercise authority over the production of the plays, taking away freedoms formerly granted to theater companies by Queen Elizabeth. Soon the King's Men learned that James

Shakespeare for Everyone to Enjoy

enjoyed their productions. James found them far superior to anything in Scotland, where he reigned before he ascended the throne of England.[20] This approval from the king brought to the King's Men a strong token of future success. It also cemented Shakespeare's place as the primary playwright in England.

During Shakespeare's final years, the records indicate that he was then involved in family life at Stratford more than ever. On June 5, 1607, the marriage of his elder daughter, Susanna, to John Hall, gentleman, was celebrated. The young groom had become a highly respected doctor of medicine in the community. He had also done well financially, and owned a large home in the neighborhood. In the next year William and Anne Shakespeare became grandparents, for the records of the parish church state that the Halls presented their newly born daughter before the parish priest for baptism on February 21, 1608. Toward the end of this same year, Will's mother, Mary, died; the parish church records her burial on September 9, 1608.[21] It is noteworthy that Mary Shakespeare was alive at the birth of her great-granddaughter.

During these final years of his career, a study of the records would indicate that Shakespeare not only continued to write and work with his theater company in various business matters, but that he also had some involvement in politics. This is documented by the fact that on September 11, 1611, the name of "Mr. William Shakespeare" appeared on the list of those contributing toward prosecuting a bill in Parliament. The subject of this bill had to do with better repair of highways.[22] This fact seems to indicate familiarity with the bad condition of the highways due to his many trips between Stratford and London.

The marriage of William and Anne's younger daughter took place on February 10, 1616. The parish register tells us that she was married to Thomas Queeny. The Shakespeares had now seen their two daughters married. However, Will's health was failing, and so on March 25, he drew up his last will and testament. As his widow, Anne was entitled to a third of the income of the estate and to continue to reside at New Place. The parish records state that William Shakespeare was buried on April 25.

The gravestone in the Stratford Church states that he died on April 23, 1616.[23] The legacy of this great playwright is incomparable, and we owe to William Shakespeare a debt of gratitude for leaving to the world the finest collection of plays ever written.

1 G. B. Harrison, *Shakespeare, Major Plays,* 1948, 8.

2 Ibid.

3 Marchette Chute, *Shakespeare of London,* N.Y.: E. P. Dutton, 1949, 13.

4 Ibid., 17.

5 Ibid., 8–20.

6 Ibid., 21–23.

7 Harrison, 1948, 8.

8 Ibid., 9.

9 Ibid.

10 Nielson and Thorndike, *The Facts about Shakespeare,* N.Y.: MacMillan, 1918, 23.

11 Ibid., 24.

12 Harrison, 1948, 10.

13 Ibid., 11.

14 Neilson and Thorndike, 25.

15 Chute, 1949, 43.

16 Harrison, 1948, 13.

17 Joseph Majault, Ed., *Shakespeare,* Geneva: Minerva, 1969, 92, 93.

18 Neilson and Thorndike, 117.

19 Harrison, *Introducing Shakespeare,* Baltimore: Penguin, 1939, 109–118.

20 Chute, 1949, 253–255.

21 Harrison, *Shakespeare, Major Plays,* 1948, 14.

22 Ibid.

23 Ibid., 15.

Chapter Four

"Converted from the World"

Shakespeare's Religion

*A*T the conclusion of his play, *As You Like It,* Shakespeare describes the conversion of a very evil man, Duke Frederick. Duke Frederick had overthrown the rightful ruler, Duke Senior, and banished him from the kingdom. Frederick had also taken the lands of Sir Rowland de Boys and put them under the control of Oliver, his eldest son. Orlando, his youngest son, is little more than a slave under a cruel master. As the play comes to a delightful conclusion, the middle son of Sir Rowland, Jaques, comes to the Forest of Arden to announce the conversion of Duke Frederick:

> I am the second son of old Sir Rowland
> That bring these tidings to this fair assembly.
> Duke Frederick, hearing how that every day
> Men of great worth resorted to this forest,
> Addressed a mighty power, which were on foot,
> In his own conduct, purposely to take
> His brother here and put him to the sword.
> And to the skirts of this wild wood he came,
> Where meeting with an old religious man,
> After some question with him, was converted
> Both from his enterprise and from the world,
> His crown bequeathing to his banished brother,
> And all their lands restored to them again
> That were with him exiled.

As You Like It, ACT V, SCENE 4, LINES 159–171

The records of Shakespeare's religion are incomplete, making it very difficult to ascertain his denominational preference. His statement of faith, found in his will, can leave no doubt that he was a strong Christian at the time of his death. However, it is far more difficult to determine which branch of Christianity he claimed, or whether he remained true to Romanism throughout his life.

Most scholars believe that Shakespeare was born a Roman Catholic and that he died a Roman Catholic. This assumption is based primarily on the belief that his father, John Shakespeare, was a confirmed Catholic who refused to join the Anglican Church. This conclusion assumes that John probably did not approve of Henry VIII's grounds for separating the Church of England from Rome. There were many Christians in England who shared this view and desired to remain in what they considered to be the only true church.

When Henry VIII desired to divorce his wife, Catharine, the Pope refused to grant his request. Men of strong Christian conscience, such as Sir Thomas More, were willing to go to the gallows rather than approve the King's demand. Henry declared himself the Head of the Church of England. This despotic act separated the Anglican Church from Rome. The Archbishop of Canterbury became the religious spokesman for the King, and there were those men in England who would not give allegiance to what they considered to be a false church. John Shakespeare is believed to be among these.

Under Queen Elizabeth, the Church of England was a compromise. England had been a Roman Catholic country until Henry VIII broke with the authority of Rome. The new church in its doctrine and ritual was not greatly changed, except that the services were read in English rather than in Latin. However, Henry VIII had caused the schism to widen when he dissolved the monasteries and abbeys and distributed the enormous wealth from their treasuries among his own followers.[1] Upheaval followed the rule of Henry VIII, especially when his daughter, Queen Mary, ascended the throne. Because she was a devout and zealous Roman Catholic, the superiority of the Pope returned for a

Shakespeare for Everyone to Enjoy

brief time. This turmoil in the religious scene was the main reason that Elizabeth wanted to establish a compromise between Roman Catholic practices and the strict Protestant doctrine, exemplified by John Knox in Scotland.

During the time of religious upheaval, England also saw the rise of two Protestant groups that would have a strong effect on religious life in England. The Puritans were the most imposing. They were zealous Christians who were committed to staying within the church to bring about reform. The Church of England was ruled by bishops and arch-bishops. Once in New England, the Puritans deduced from their study of the Scriptures a system of church government that started with the authority of elders elected by every local congregation.[2]

Because the Puritan believed that a Christian nation is a Christian church, he was a Nationalist. He demanded that the Anglican Church be thoroughly reformed. The Puritan was motivated by his strong faith that the Bible taught him to insist that there be right government in both church and state. He further believed that he had a moral responsibility not only to live by God's standards, but also to compel other men to live by these same standards.[3]

The Puritan was also a Scripturist who promoted the moral principles of the Bible as the only rule of faith and practice. The Puritan searched the Scriptures to find precise arrangements of public administration, which led him to be guided by the Bible's teaching on minutest points of individual conduct.[4] This attitude and forceful presence brought to the Puritan a degree of public ridicule and persecution.

The Puritans were often recognized by their stark dress and their open criticism of lax morality. Queen Elizabeth and her supporters found these views to be alarming and revolutionary, especially when some Anglicans believed the Puritans were trying to force everyone to conform to their standards. This led to periods of persecution for those who claimed to follow Puritan views.

Nevertheless, the Puritan influence made its mark on England, and certainly Shakespeare experienced some degree of influence from their teachings. Because the Puritans opposed the theaters, especially those in London, their influence may also have had a negative force against the playwright's work in the theater. However, we have no record that Shakespeare or his company suffered from the Puritan attempts to close down the London playhouses.

Another influential religous group were the Separatists (known to us as Pilgrims), differing radically from the Puritans who primarily sought to reform from within the Church. The Pilgrims believed they should "reform without tarrying for any," and therefore separated themselves from the Church of England. The Pilgrim refused to follow the Anglican Prayerbook, and wanted total freedom from Queen Elizabeth's episcopacy. It was the Pilgrims who proclaimed, "No king but Jesus!" Their greatest desire was for liberty for themselves, their families, and their brothers in Christ.[5] The Pilgrims endured persecution from the leaders of the Church of England.

Toward the end of Shakespeare's career, a small group of Separatists fled to Holland because of this intense persecution. They also desired to secure liberty to walk with God according to the dictates of conscience. While still in Holland, the Pilgrims established a congregational form of government in their church through the wise guidance of their pastor, the Rev. John Robinson. He was convinced that church decisions should be vested in the congregation rather than in the elders. He also taught them the importance of liberty of conscience and to live peaceably with those who disagreed with them. In 1620, this band of Pilgrims sailed to America and founded Plymouth Colony in a new territory, first called the northern parts of Virginia, later called New England. They were kind and helpful to the struggling Puritan colony of Massachusetts Bay founded later.

"American self-government was not the sudden birth of the Declaration of Independence. . . . It really sprang from the organisation which the Pilgrim Fathers gave to the first colony, an organisation which determined the shape and character of the State Constitutions which followed."[6] Both the Puritan and the Pilgrim had a profound influence on the shaping of New England's government and the formation of the

Constitution of the United States of America. Although the Separatists never established a foothold in the government of England, during the 1600s the Puritans managed to seize control of the civil power under Cromwell. The fact that these forces were at work during his lifetime would indicate that this religious upheaval had at least an indirect effect on the life and work of William Shakespeare. It is also important to note that he wrote his plays in a political atmosphere that was reacting to these religious forces.

There is also evidence that the Shakespeare family had made contacts with the Puritan movement. When William married Anne Hathaway in 1582, he married a woman whose father probably had some Puritan leanings. Years later, documents supporting Puritan theology were found hidden in the thatch roof of the Hathaway cottage. Anne Hathaway's father, Richard, stated in his will, that he wanted to be "honestly buried," which was a Puritan phrase. It is also interesting that William and Anne named their first child Susanna, a name not common in the Stratford area at that time, but much favored by the Puritans.[7]

On June 5, 1607, Susanna was given in marriage to a prominent Puritan physician, Dr. John Hall, an Oxford graduate and a member of the local gentry. Dr. Hall was such an able physician that his Puritan leanings did not harm his practice; to the contrary, his honest and straightforward character helped him to gain great fame for his skill. He soon became the most respected and trusted physician in Stratford.[8]

The tradition that William Shakespeare never joined the Church of England but followed his father's loyalty to Catholicism is based on strong evidence that both the Arden and Shakespeare families were reticent to change their loyalty. Edward Oakes says that this evidence is "direct and overwhelming."[9] Shakespeare's mother, Mary Arden, was born into one of the most prominent and zealous Catholic families in Warwickshire. In fact, Edward Arden, the head of the Arden clan, hired a gardener who was actually his own private Roman priest in disguise.[10]

The recorded facts linking William Shakespeare to the Catholic denomination are too many for this discussion, but one fact needs to be included. William and Anne were not married in the local Stratford church, but in Temple Grafton (five miles away) by the Catholic vicar of the village. Although some scholars believe that Shakespeare eventually joined the Church of England, based on the fact that he is buried in the Anglican Church in Stratford, a seventeenth-century Anglican archdeacon from nearby Coventry reported: "according to Stratford oral tradition, Shakespeare died a papist."[11]

The most important evidence for Shakespeare's personal faith is found in his last will and testament. Here he wrote one of the most concise expressions of the Christian faith: "First, I commend my soul into the hands of God my Creator, hoping and assuredly believing, through the only merits of Jesus Christ my Savior, to be made partaker of life everlasting."[12] Although some scholars believe he became a Christian in his later years, there is far more evidence that he was born into a Christian family and that he remained a Christian throughout his life.

Whatever else is known about Shakespeare's religion, it is abundantly clear from studying his plays that he knew the Bible well. All his plays testify to this fact, for they are filled with Scriptural principles and allusions. Since the King James Bible was not translated until 1611, the Bible frequently used in his day was the Geneva Bible. In all probability, this was the translation used by Shakespeare. Ernest Howse, in supporting this view, states: "He knew the Bible so well, that in hundreds, indeed in thousands, of his passages we can trace its phraseology, and beyond its phraseology we can trace its thought."[13]

One more interesting note is found in a careful study of Psalm 46, which I now call the "Shakespeare Psalm." In the King James Version of the Bible, go to Psalm 46. Count down, from the beginning of the psalm, forty-six words. You will find that the forty-sixth word is "shake." Then go to the end of the psalm, and count up forty-six words from the last word, and you will find the forty-sixth word is "spear." Shakespeare was well known to the Bible scholars of his day. Since the King James translation was developed by a large group of scholars, perhaps they arranged

Shakespeare for Everyone to Enjoy

the order of these two words in such a way as to honor the great playwright. Others say that Shakespeare, who was 46 years old at the time, may have been asked to help with the poetic phrasing of the psalms, and "signed" the 46th Psalm. The King James Bible was completed in 1611, just five years before William Shakespeare's death.

The more that scholars delve into the depths of Shakespeare's characters, plots, and the underlying principles of his work, the easier it is for them to conclude that Shakespeare's knowledge of Scripture surpassed that of many preachers. The most powerful experiences in drama occur in his great plays, which he produced at the height of his career. We discover the reason for the great success of these plays when we realize that the main issues of human life as portrayed by Shakespeare occur, not for an age, but for all time.[13]

Many critics have defended the view that Shakespeare was not a Christian based on speculation that he lived most of his life in London, separated from his family in Stratford, and on other traditions which cannot be supported by facts. My conclusion is based on his statement of faith and all the records that have been found. There is no concrete evidence to prove that he was not a Christian. As to his denominational attachment to the Roman Catholic Church, it is my personal belief that he kept his membership in that church out of loyalty to his father and mother. His plays not only reveal his profound understanding of Holy Scripture, but they also demonstrate his primary commitment to the commands of Christ.

Undoubtedly, as the excerpt below shows, he began his will with a concise statement of faith because he wanted to make it crystal clear to his family and loved ones that he would be in heaven, not because of anything he had done, but because of Christ's death on the cross.

> [F]irst, I comend my soule into the handes of God my Creator, hoping and assuredlie beleeving, through thonelie merittes, of Jesus Christe my Saviour, to be made partaker of lyfe everlastinge. . . .
>
> —Shakespeare's Will, Appendix II, 121

1 G. B. Harrison, *Shakespeare, Major Plays*, 1948, 22.

2 Ibid.

3 Verna M. Hall, *The Christian History of the Constitution of the United States of America*, Vol. I: *Christian Self-Government*, San Francisco: Foundation for American Christian Education, 1966 & subsequent editions from Chesapeake, VA, 182.

4 Ibid., 48.

5 Ibid., 182.

6 John Brown, B.A., D.D. *The Pilgrim Fathers of New England and Their Puritan Successors*, 1895; Republished: Pasadena, Texas: Pilgrim Publications, 1970, 16.

7 Marchette Chute, *Shakespeare of London*, NY: E. P. Dutton, 1949, 53.

8 Ibid., 195.

9 Edward T. Oakes, "Shakespeare's Millennium," *First Things*, Dec. 1999, 18.

10 Ibid.

11 Ibid., 19.

12 Neilson and Thorndike, *The Facts about Shakespeare*, NY: MacMillan, 1922, 208.

13 Ernest Marshall Howse, *Spiritual Values in Shakespeare*, NY: Abingdon, 1955, 10.

14 Ibid., 16.

Chapter Five

"Conscience Is the Most Sacred of All Property"
James Madison

The Principle Approach® to Shakespeare[1]

*T*HE serious student will conclude that Shakespeare's plays are based on principles. The basis for these principles is found in the Bible. As I pointed out in the last chapter, Shakespeare knew the Bible in depth. This knowledge gave him the tools to apply Biblical principles to life with all its failures and successes. Broken principles lead to tragic results, often leading to death, or to comic episodes in both ordinary and unusual circumstances. Shakespeare's characters who followed Biblical principles often achieved results far above expectation. I will illustrate this in a later chapter.

First, it is important for us to understand the Principle Approach® to education. In my years of teaching Shakespeare, I followed this method set forth by Rosalie Slater. She said: "The Principle Approach® begins by restoring the 4-Rs to teaching and learning." [2] These 4-Rs are: researching, reasoning, relating, and recording. By having each student follow this method, he is able to reach his own conclusions and learn how to apply Biblical principles to his own life and situation.

This is an excellent method for guiding the student into a deeper appreciation of both Shakespeare and the Bible. Just as Shakespeare researched God's Word to identify basic principles, a serious student will likewise find these principles in reading a play. After researching God's Word, the student begins to reason from the principle to a point of understanding that allows him to easily identify that same principle in the play he is studying. Students who have been researching and reasoning from Biblical principles for several years will find an excitement in their first studies of Shakespeare that students who lack this training may not experience.

The relating of Biblical principles to plot, characters, or other aspects of any of Shakespeare's plays will follow naturally for these students. My first experience in teaching the play *As You Like It* to a class of juniors and seniors, in which most of the students had been using the Principle Approach® in their studies since grade school, was for me a revelation. Never before had I experienced such excitement and love for Shakespeare without any attempt on my part to create such enthusiasm.

Because these students had followed the 4-R method for many years, they quite naturally recorded their personal reactions in their notebooks. I could not believe the insights some of them noted each day! Their enjoyment rubbed off on those new students who had recently enrolled in the school. I didn't even have to convince them of the importance of doing all of the work or following the methodology in detail. In fact, the students' own insights recorded in their notebooks became the material for our class discussions.

The enthusiasm for the play grew daily, to the point that, one day, a student raised his hand and said, "Mr. Brown, we want to put this play on the stage. We want to produce it for our class play next spring." My first thought at that moment was, "Dr. Angus Bowmer, we need you now!" After I collected my thoughts, I responded, "I will direct this play if you can find me a producer and a stage. I want the play produced on our campus, and the only room large enough is the church sanctuary. We will need a portable stage that can be set up during the week and removed for the weekend so that the church members will not have their worship disturbed by our school production."

The students not only located and secured an outstanding and loyal producer, but one of the boys in the class designed the stage, organized a group to build it, and set up a construction crew to put it up and take it down during the final weeks of rehearsal and production. Rarely have I seen this kind of dedication to Shakespeare, especially among a group of students who had never previously studied his plays. The 4-R method requires time and patience for both teachers and students. Although I had been teaching Shakespeare classes for over fifteen years, this was only my second year to use the Principle Approach®. This event alone convinced me that the Principle Approach to teaching, as identified and restored from America's founding period, was worth all the time and personal struggle demanded of both teachers and students.

In a later chapter, I will relate my experiences in directing *As You Like It*, but now it is expedient for me to explain more about how the Principle Approach® may be used in the study of Shakespeare. For many people, Shakespeare is thought to be dry and difficult to understand, primarily because of the language. However, when a student has the tools to look for principles, he begins to realize the impact of these plays on his own life.

Let us return to another quote from Rosalie Slater: "The Principle Approach® is America's historic Christian method of Biblical reasoning, which makes the Truths of God's Word the basis of every subject in the school curriculum."[3] A scholar always begins his work with his own research. A scholar who accepts the Bible as truth has in his hand a treasure chest of knowledge and he can use this knowledge as a basis for reasoning and to identify subjects he desires to study. Because Shakespeare had learned that the Bible was the basis of all human knowledge as well as a book that contains every human experience, both good and evil, and because he was taught the principles of logic and reason, he had a platform upon which he could build the plots and characters of his plays.

Shakespeare was so gifted with the ability to relate these principles to the development of his plays that any audience could identify with a character and follow the plot through the failures or successes of that particular character. His comedies show this principle more than his tragedies, since audiences who identify with certain comic situations find themselves laughing at their own shortcomings. But even in the tragedies, we find ourselves identifying with a tragic figure, especially one who displays our own failures. Hamlet comes to mind, for he cannot bring himself to action that is immediately required. Most of us have times in our life when we cannot make an important decision. Like Hamlet, we find it easier to let circumstances cause the problem to become more complicated, with unpleasant results.

Shakespeare would have developed his plot and sub-plots, woven together the characters he had invented for a particular play into some incredible relationships, and also added material from many other sources, such as Greek and Roman mythology, previously written plays, settings from other cultures, or even inferences to contemporary events. He could understand and sympathize with his audience more than any other dramatist. G. B. Harrison states: "He can see the whole picture of humanity and re-create it so that men of every kind, country, creed, and generation understand."[4]

The Principle Approach® to education, as developed by Rosalie Slater, begins with the Bible. God's providential hand is seen in history and in God's relationship and purpose expressed through nations and individuals. The works of Shakespeare demonstrate this theme, especially in his history plays. When the plays are studied in historical order, the hand of God will be seen moving characters and events through a predestined plan. The play, *Henry V*, dramatically illustrates this principle. Before the Battle of Agincourt, in which the French troops outnumber the English five to one, Henry prays for his troops to meet the challenge. When the battle is over, the English have won victoriously, with only small losses to their number.

Rosalie Slater taught the Bible as the "source and seedbed of literature," exemplifying the literary types such as narrative, drama, history, and poetry. The Bible in English is the greatest English language classic, and the works of Shakespeare second. In the framework of God's providential history, "literature is the hand maid of history."

So in the Principle Approach® to studying Shakespeare, his life, the setting, the content, and his influence all have historical as well as aesthetic significance. In Shakespeare's time, the course of history is dramatically affected by the Bible in the hands of the individual. The quickening affect on individual conscience is dramatically revealed in Shakespeare's plays. Plus the seeds of civil liberty planted in the Reformation and illustrated in literature contributed to the English preparation for individual and civil liberty in America.[5]

Researching and reasoning from the Bible and history is invaluable for a serious student in deriving principles from Shakespeare's plays. Principles such as individuality, character, self-government, conscience, property, and union are all found in the works of Shakespeare.

One of the traits that demonstrate the genius of Shakespeare is his ability to construct the details for each character development. Because he had an uncanny understanding of the individuality of each person, his plays are filled with unique and delightful personalities. Furthermore, through his characters, Shakespeare continually reminds us of our own experiences so that we easily identify with them in their successes or failures. Hamlet, Cordelia, Lear, Portia, or Brutus, all seek our empathy. Even very minor characters, such as the Boy in *Henry V*, or Adam in *As You Like It* have memorable qualities.

Characters who are blessed with a certain amount of self-government, such as Viola in *Twelfth Night*, or Antonio in *Merchant of Venice*, in spite of difficulties along the way, end with success. Those who lack self-government usually fail to find success or meet with tragedy. Romeo becomes a tragic figure because he allows his infatuation for Juliet to overcome his ability to rule his passions. Macbeth, who seems to be in full control of himself at the beginning of the play, is lured, first by the prophesies of the witches, and then by his domineering wife, so that he ends his life tragically having lost control of his mind.

Generally, those persons who have character traits identified with Biblical teaching, or who gain them during the course of the drama, rise to the occasion and claim the admiration of the audience. Shakespeare's depiction of King Henry V is a prime example. When three traitors are brought before him for judgment, Henry gives them the opportunity to repent so their souls may be saved from Hell, but they must still face the death penalty for their crime. King Henry is a great general in war, but he also spends the night before the battle walking among his troops in the guise of an ordinary soldier, encouraging his officers and troops. Then he goes to prayer for their safety, courage, and victory. He governs his people with truth and justice. This is in contrast with kings such as: Richard II, who stole property from landowners and levied heavy taxes on the poor; or Richard III, who murdered everyone in his path, including children, to become king.

On the matter of conscience, no one stands out clearer than Hamlet. We headed this chapter with a quote from James Madison: "Conscience is the most sacred of all property." Property is both internal and external. The internal property of conscience guides everyone toward his external actions. Hamlet has been told by his father (in the form of a Ghost) to kill his uncle. Claudius has murdered his brother, taken his throne, and married his widow, Hamlet's mother. Hamlet's problem is one of indecision and procrastination. The more he delays, the worse the situation becomes. When Hamlet is considering suicide in his famous soliloquy, "To be, or not to be," he ends his thoughts with the following: "Thus conscience doth make cowards of us all, and thus the native hue of resolution . . . and enterprises of great pitch and movement . . . lose the name of action."[6]

Many scholars have recognized and identified principles in their study of Shakespeare and his works. Ernest Howse is one of those scholars. He believes that beneath the surface of Shakespeare's works are Biblical principles, although the audience or reader of the play may not see an overt connection with specific Scripture. In fact, some of his plays may not contain anything specifically Biblical on the surface, but a careful reading will reveal the most important issues of human life that underlie the script. These issues or principles of human life, so common in the great plays of Shakespeare, are not for an age, but for all time.[7]

Too often these principles are lost in a simplistic reading of a play. I have attended a few performances of Shakespeare's plays that were so bad, I wondered if either the actors or the director understood the play. The underlying message or theme was lost in the midst of a setting contrary to

Shakespeare for Everyone to Enjoy

the playwright's original intent, or the acting simply did not have enough resolve for the audience to follow the plot. By taking out Shakespeare's ingenious designs, the beauty of the work is destroyed. Not only is the original message lost, but also the production appears boring, hard to understand, and rife with political correctness.

Performing Shakespearean plays true to the master, Angus Bowmer, founder of the Oregon Shakespeare Festival at Ashland, Oregon, projected to the audience the powerful messages of the plays. He learned this technique from B. Iden Payne, who was at that time the Guest Director at the University of Washington.[8] What impressed Dr. Bowmer the most about Payne's Shakespeare productions was the thrill of seeing the plays set on the type of stage for which they were written. Bowmer goes on to say about Payne: "I do not refer to the values any young actor receives from contact with a great director and teacher, but to those impressions, attitudes, prejudices (if you will) toward Shakespeare's scripts in relationship to their presentation on an Elizabethan stage garnered from my association with Iden Payne."[9]

It was Dr. Bowmer's dream to produce Shakespeare on the Elizabethan stage. In 1947, the festival in Ashland built its second stage on the grounds of the old Chautauqua building. This stage was adequate for Elizabethan productions, but still did not have the grandeur of the stages of the late 1500s in London. In 1959, the second stage was torn down to make room for a real Elizabethan theater. This magnificent stage was patterned after the Fortune of Shakespeare's time and would remind the audience of Shakespeare's Globe. Richard Hay, who was the brilliant designer of this new stage, also was most eager to replace the lighting board with a new switchboard that had just come on the market.[9]

In 1970, an indoor theater was built next to the Elizabethan theater, which is called the Angus Bowmer Theatre. Dr. Bowmer told me that the plans were to produce Elizabethan plays, often in Elizabethan costume, on the outdoor stage and to use the indoor theater for other plays by a great variety of playwrights and for experimental Shakespearean performances. Later the Black Swan was established for plays "in the round" where the audience is close to the stage. A few years ago, the Black Swan was closed, and a larger, state-of-the-art, theater (called the New Theatre) was built.

I have been fortunate to attend at least one performance of every Shakespeare play produced by the Oregon Shakespeare Festival since 1969. The Elizabethan theater with the period costumes has been a real motivation for directors to draw the best actors to Ashland. In this atmosphere it is much easier for audiences to follow the plot and glean from the production the principles and themes that Shakespeare has woven into his plays. I am convinced that Ashland offers some of the best Shakespeare in America, especially for those audiences who want to experience Shakespeare the way he wrote and produced his plays.

---

1 The Principle Approach® is the publisher's trademark for Rosalie J. Slater's teachings derived from America's Christian History, as published in her work, *Teaching and Learning America's Christian History: The Principle Approach*®, 1965, published by The Foundation for American Christian Education, P.O. Box 9588, Chesapeake, VA 23321. Rosalie J. Slater, co-founder, also authored *The Noah Plan*® *Literature Curriculum Guide: The Principle Approach® Kindergarten through Twelfth Grade*, San Francisco: Foundation for American Christian Education, 1977, and on pages 147–190, she presents a complete curriculum and resources list for teaching Shakespeare as "The Bard of the Bible." See Appendix V for more about, The Principle Approach® and The Foundation for American Christian Education.

2 Rosalie J. Slater, *Teaching and Learning America's Christian History: The Principle Approach*®, San Francisco: Foundation for American Christian Education, 1973 & subsequent editions from Chesapeake, VA, 88.

3 Ibid.

4 G. B. Harrison, "The Universality of Shakespeare," *Shakespeare, Major Plays*, N.Y.: Harcourt, Brace, 1948, 3.

5 Slater.

6 *Hamlet*, Act III, scene 1, lines 83–88.

7 Ernest Marshall Howse, *Spiritual Values in Shakespeare*, N.Y.: Abingdon, 1955, 16–18.

8 Angus L. Bowmer, *As I Remember, Adam*, Ashland, Oregon: The Oregon Shakespeare Festival Association, 1975, 25.

9 Ibid., 31–32.

10 Ibid., 244–251.

Chapter Six

"And Man Became a Living Soul"
(Genesis 2:7)

Spiritual Values in Shakespeare's Plays

CLOSELY related to Biblical principles are spiritual values. In the early development of drama, especially in ancient Greece, religion was the underlying element of plays. Elizabethan drama underwent a rebirth that was likewise rooted in religion; for its predecessor, medieval drama, began in the Church. Ernest Howse believes that "religion created drama, nourished it, imbued it with dignity and purpose; and drama grew up to be religion's prodigal daughter."[1] The majority of the plays that the Elizabethan stage brought to its culture departed from this heritage. Writers such as Marlowe, Jonson, and Shakespeare, however, began producing plays that soared to a peak in the history of drama. The significant difference between the works of Marlowe, Jonson, and Shakespeare and of some of their contemporaries is in their ability to weave spiritual values into their plots and characters.

The works of Shakespeare are not ecclesiastical, but do often reflect Biblical themes. Drama is often not based on anything specifically from the Bible, nor make any mention of God or Christ, since it has been produced for the secular stage. The key is found in the essential marks that display religious values, which are seen in the kinds of choices and the quality of insight the dramatist has written into his play. "Often drama may . . . be of the very texture of Christian thought, so that it would be impossible to imagine its being produced save in a culture influenced by the Hebrew prophets and Jesus."[2]

Because Shakespeare's plays are sprinkled with these spiritual values, the audience will find truth, beauty, and goodness. Life, however marred, is not seen to be contemptible or futile, but infinite and promising, even in the most tragic circumstances. Victor Hugo understood how this factor led to Shakespeare's greatness when he stated: "England has two books: one which she made; the other which made her—Shakespeare and the Bible."[3] Part of Shakespeare's genius is found in his innate ability to intertwine the values of Scripture into his plays to the extent that audiences are not overtly aware of them. It is only through an in-depth study of Shakespeare's character development that these values are fully revealed.

As I stated above, the majority of Shakespearean plays do not have specifically Biblical themes. Only two plays have themes directly related to Scripture: *Measure for Measure* and *As You Like It*. The former actually takes its title from Scripture: "For with what judgment ye judge, ye shall be judged; and with what measure ye mete, it shall be measured to you again."[4] The theme for the latter play is found in Act V, where Jaques De Boys announces: "Duke Frederick . . . where meeting with an old religious man, after some question with him, was converted both from his enterprise and from the world, his crown bequeathing to his banished brother, and all their lands restored to them again that were with him exiled."[5] The theme is reinforced by Jaques (a Lord of the banished Duke) who states: "Out of these convertites [converts to the religious life] there is much matter to be heard and learned."[6]

Although the theme of *King Lear,* the tragic consequences of ingratitude, is not Biblical in the same manner as the two plays mentioned above, *Lear* is filled with Scriptural values. In fact, Edward T. Oakes believes that the British writer Germaine Greer is correct in asserting that *Lear* is the most Christian of all Shakespeare's plays.[7] The basis for Greer's insight is found in the role of the Fool, who becomes the catalyst for Lear's dynamic change. Lear is converted from a vain and arrogant man in Act I. He is changed to a penitent and merciful soul through undergoing increasing torment and suffering.

Shakespeare for Everyone to Enjoy

Most of Shakespeare's fools lead men toward understanding and wisdom, but the Fool of *King Lear* is especially gifted in assisting Lear to interpret the reasons for his suffering. This Fool also leads Lear from his former tyrannical failure to use his power in responsible ways, to a life of justice. In the midst of the storm, the Fool causes Lear to think about those poor souls he had forsaken in the days of his totalitarian rule. It is the Fool that makes Lear aware of his two evil daughters, who are not honoring him but taking away his imperial rights. Then, finally, it is his loyal daughter, Cordelia, who awakens in her father the truth about his former life. Lear exclaims, "You must bear with me. Pray you now, forget and forgive, I am old and foolish."[8]

This transformation of character does not happen to Lear alone. Throughout Act III, all of the good characters are improving in goodness through their unfortunate circumstances and resulting intense suffering. At the same time, the evil people in the play are becoming hardened in their wicked intent to bring suffering upon Lear, Gloucester, and Edgar for their success in achieving increasing amounts of power. The play begins to turn from its tragic theme to a tone of prophetic quality. The evildoers have been adept at spreading misery and destruction all around them; yet by the end of the play, evil itself produces destruction. The transformation of the character of the once-ungrateful king into a man who repents of his former sins awakens in the audience a realization that it is better to have one devoted and loyal daughter, dead in Lear's arms, than the two ungrateful daughters, dead by their own wickedness.[9]

As Lear gains insight into his previous weaknesses, he develops a deep concern for the forgotten men of the world: the homeless and the hungry. More and more he is able to see the torment of those who suffer under tyranny. This attitude in Lear caused Germaine Greer to refute the view of George Orwell that Shakespeare favored the rich and famous. Greer concludes: "The Fool's comments in *Lear* indicate how deeply Christian Shakespeare remained throughout his writing career."[10]

Moral values are revealed in both good and evil character. In fact, spirituality is the essential ingredient that moves men to Christian growth, and Shakespeare is gifted in developing characters that demonstrate morality as well as immorality. The one sure result in Shakespearean drama is that moral principles are guiding forces for good, while immorality leads to undesired consequences.

An immoral character may achieve success for most of the play, but in the end he suffers and often dies. Lady Macbeth has a hardness which her husband lacks. Macbeth, whose character is a mixture of good and evil qualities, succumbs to her persistence to murder those who stand in his way to become King. The weakness in Macbeth's character keeps him from breaking free from the power of his wife, who knows and can easily exploit his evil side.

In *Macbeth*, Shakespeare uses the setting of a play to instill in the audience a sense of the presence of evil. The play begins with the suggestions of the Witches, who in Elizabethan times were accepted by most people as real and very wicked. These Witches were evil women who had trafficked with the devil and had been given strange powers and supernatural knowledge. Because of the prophecies of the Witches, Macbeth receives his first external temptation. When his ambitious wife hears of the prophecies, she begins to weave together a plot to make them come true.

After Macbeth murders Duncan, King of Scotland, he proceeds to carry out a series of murders to put him on the throne of Scotland. "From this point onward, the tragedy is splashed with blood. Once the murder has been committed, the blood of Duncan drips down the stairs after Macbeth until it pervades the whole universe, and he stands alone in a universal sea of blood."[11] The difference between the reactions of Macbeth and Lady Macbeth is striking. Macbeth is completely overcome by the realization that he has committed a heinous sin, but his wife is merely concerned about the details for carrying out the next steps of action. She thinks that a little water is all she needs to wash her hands, but Macbeth knows he can never find enough water to be clean again. He cries out, "Will all great Neptune's ocean wash this blood clean from my hand? No, this my hand will rather the multitudinous seas incarnadine,[12] making the green one red."[13]

The drama continues to weave a web of murder and deceit until at last Lady Macbeth comes to the realization that even she cannot get the spot of blood out of her life. She is observed continuing to wash her hands for as long as a quarter hour. When Macbeth is told of his queen's death, he responds with his famous speech that ends: "It (life) is a tale told by an idiot, full of sound and fury, signifying nothing."[14] Macbeth is killed in battle by Macduff, whose wife and children had previously been murdered by Macbeth's command. Thus good triumphs over evil.

Spiritual values are found in the entire Shakespearean canon. However, they are found more prominently in some plays than others. One time a fellow teacher asked me, "How can you possibly find any spiritual values in *A Midsummer Night's Dream*?" That was a good question, because, at first glance, there appears to be none. During the summer of 2003, we attended a superb production of this play in Ashland, Oregon; in fact, the director used such a magical setting that even the hardest of hearts was melted. The secret was in the atmosphere of an enchanted forest, where the beauty of imminent conjugal love was fully revealed. The ending of the play left the audience with a strong statement for the exalted and enduring value of the institution of Christian marriage.

The joy of studying the works of Shakespeare and then attending performances that are thoughtfully and carefully put on the stage is difficult to impart to people who have not had this experience. I strongly encourage you, the reader, to get involved so that you can also taste the satisfaction found when an outstanding performance is given. The more you experience this, the more you will begin to see the spiritual values in Shakespeare's plays.

Another factor that Shakespeare used to demonstrate spiritual matters is money or wealth. The problems that result from borrowing money are presented in one of Shakespeare's best-known plays, *The Merchant of Venice*. Antonio is a wealthy businessman. His dear friend Bassanio asks him for a loan of enough money to go to Belmont and seek Portia's hand in marriage. Since the entirety of Antonio's funds are tied up in his merchant ships, all of which are at sea, he must find some means of securing the desired sum before his ships return to Venice.

The immediate solution to this predicament is found in a proposed loan from a Jewish moneylender. At this point, Shakespeare introduces his audience to one of his most fascinating characters. Shylock already has a dim view of Antonio, whom Shylock considers to be his enemy. After all, he says that Antonio spat on him last week and at another time called him a dog. Why should Shylock lend money to a man who has nothing but contempt for the Jew? At this juncture, the drama takes on a different twist. Shylock will lend this large sum of money to Antonio for a most inhumane bond, a pound of Antonio's flesh, to be cut off and taken from whatever part of Antonio's body Shylock chooses.

The plot unfolds as Antonio loses all of his ships, and the bond must be paid. This shows clearly why God desires his followers to listen to His instructions. The Bible teaches the dangers that arise from being in debt. Even the foolish Polonius advises his son to be neither borrower nor lender in the play, *Hamlet*. But in the *The Merchant of Venice*, Shakespeare builds Shylock's character around a theme much worse than the futility of indebtedness. Shylock has taken on the greater sin of man's inhumanity to man. At last Portia, disguised as a lawyer, convinces the court to free Antonio from his bond. Shylock is then stripped of his family, his fortune, and his faith.

Shylock leaves the stage as neither hero nor villain. Throughout the play, even though Shylock has a contemptuous spirit, the audience is sympathetic to his plight. This is a comedy, and Shakespeare never intended for this story to be taken too seriously. He certainly was not trying to present an anti-Semitic theme, as some have charged. In a way, *Merchant* is more than comedy, for there is in this play a strong desire for justice for both the Christian and the Jew.[15]

The above examples have been presented to give the reader insight into Shakespeare's methodology for constructing his plots and characters. Although Shakespeare may not have always deliberately set out to build these spiritual values into his plays in the same way that he intentionally formed his themes, the finished products reveal many religious insights to students who search the heart of Shakespeare's works. As I pointed out in a previous chapter, William Shakespeare had gained such a thorough knowledge of Scripture that he subconsciously wove the threads of Scripture into each of his plays in a most intriguing way. I have found no other playwright whose works demonstrate such a command of Scripture, and therefore produce such a profound religious effect.

1 Ernest Marshall Howse, *Spiritual Values in Shakespeare*, N.Y.: Abingdon, 1955, 16.

2 Ibid., 18.

3 Victor Hugo, *William Shakespeare*, London: Hurst and Blackett, 1864, 312.

4 Matthew 7:2, King James Version (hereafter KJV).

5 *As You Like It*, Act V, scene 4, lines 160–171, (all line numbering is from the Harrison text, *Major Plays*, since numbering varies because of textual differences ued by other editors).

6 Ibid., lines 190–191.

7 Edward T. Oakes, "Shakespeare's Millennium," *First Things*, Dec. 1999, 19.

8 *King Lear*, Act IV, scene 7, lines 84–85.

9 Howse, 70–71.

10 Oakes, 19.

11 G. B. Harrison, ed., *Shakespeare, Major Plays*, 1948, 832.

12 *incarnadine*: "make red."

13 *Macbeth*, Act II, scene 2, lines 60–64.

14 Ibid., Act V, scene 5, lines 26–28.

15 Howse, 120.

Chapter Seven

"Don't Ride the Green Bus"

A Visit to Stratford-on-Avon

*I*N late summer, 1999, my wife and I rode the train from London to Stratford-upon-Avon along with two of our adult sons, David and Mark, and two teen-age family friends, Angela and Amy Chamberlain. As we approached Stratford, we were discussing some of the sights we were planning to see. The man in the seat in front of us jumped up and told us: "Don't ride the green bus! The guides will tell you false statements about William Shakespeare, stories that are based on pure conjecture. If you want to get the truth, visit the various family homes, and the docents will give you documented facts."

When we arrived in Stratford, we bypassed the green bus and stopped at the tourist office to get maps and information. Since we did not want to ride the green bus, we decided to walk. Our first stop was the Hathaway cottage in the village of Shottery. This is probably the best known of the houses in the Stratford area, the cottage where Shakespeare's wife, Anne, was raised.

We were somewhat surprised that the house was called a cottage, because it was actually quite large. In Elizabethan days, the Hathaway cottage was in the country outside the town limits. In fact, it was a rather lengthy walk from the Hathaway cottage to the center of Stratford. Today, the town has grown so large that it appears that the Hathaway home is within the town of Stratford. However, the property is extensive, and once you enter the gate, there is a country atmosphere.

After spending some time in the gardens, we entered the home and were greeted by a very well-informed docent. She told us many facts and stories that have been documented about the Hathaway family and cottage. We learned that Anne Hathaway's father died the year before she was married to William Shakespeare, and that he left her a marriage portion in his will. Anne was the eldest daughter by her father's first marriage and was twenty-five when her father made his will. Also her brother, Bartholomew, also married almost immediately after the death of their father.

The docent continued to explain some of the details concerning Anne and William's marriage. Even though William was very young, it was most likely that Anne's father had worked out arrangements for their marriage before he died. Long before the marriage ceremony, the parents had agreed upon a pre-contract, which was almost as binding as the marriage itself. The pre-contract would have been signed by the couple to be wed and by both sets of parents. These facts corroborated what I had learned from other sources as recorded in chapter three of this book.

At this point, I asked the docent about the materials that had been discovered in the thatch of the roof when the old roof was being replaced. She explained that she had not actually seen these papers, but had been informed that they contained information about the Hathaway family and their relationship to the Puritan movement. She strongly asserted that the family not only had held definite ties to the Puritan beliefs, but that they were concerned that Anne should marry into a family that held no prejudice against these beliefs. The docent said that although John Shakespeare was known to be a devout Catholic, she was not aware of any information that would indicate the Shakespeare family held specific prejudice toward the Puritans. She was also of the opinion that Will's father had proposed the idea of a future marriage between Anne and his son several years earlier.

A discussion arose in the group touring the Hathaway cottage. One person said he was concerned about the fact that Susanna, William and Anne's first child, was born the following May, though the marriage ceremony had been performed the previous November. The docent informed us that this question is often raised when people tour the Hathaway cottage. The docent also explained that in Elizabethan times, the custom was to consider a pre-contract almost as binding as we consider the marriage itself. She concluded these remarks by telling us: "The seven months between a marriage and the birth of a child would not have been questioned or considered morally unacceptable to the people of Stratford in those days."

In Elizabethan times, Anne Hathaway's cottage was known as Hewlands. Richard, her father, was a farmer, and the house remained as a working farm until the 1800s. The Hathaway family lived in the house for 300 years. The farmhouse was built in two main stages. During the first stage, about two-thirds of the present building was completed, having been constructed in the mid-fifteenth century. This was probably the extent of the house when Anne was growing up. The taller section was built onto the existing structure in the seventeenth century. Bartholomew Hathaway, Anne's eldest brother, who inherited the house when his father died, probably built on the second stage. In 1892, the Shakespeare Birthplace Trust purchased the Hathaway cottage so that they could oversee its permanent preservation and have it open to the public.[1]

The docent concluded her tour with two anecdotes from the Elizabethan farm community. She explained how many of the families were too poor to afford a dining table, and would therefore take two sawhorses and place a large board over them to form a table. Most of the family members sat on benches around the table, but at the head of the table was a chair, usually for the father. Sometimes grange meetings were held around this table. The president of the grange sat on the chair, and he became "the chairman of the board."

The second anecdote concerned the use of straw and hay on the dirt floors to keep them warmer. Sometimes the hay (thresh) would be too bulky under the door. It was necessary to put a board over the hay in the doorway so that the door could be closed. This board was the "threshold." The groom would carry his bride over this threshold when the couple entered their home after the wedding.

Our next stop was at a mansion known as Hall's Croft. This is the home where Shakespeare's eldest daughter, Susanna and her husband, Dr. John Hall, lived. Dr. Hall was one of the most successful physicians in Elizabethan England. Extensive displays of his medical instruments, herbs, drugs, and medicines in the exhibition room, detail the doctor's life and practice. His reputation as a doctor spread far beyond Stratford. After Dr. Hall died, his medical notes were published in a book, which describes the many and diverse illnesses he treated as well as the methods of treatment he used.[2]

The home of Dr. and Mrs. John Hall is a beautiful, fine-timbered building on Old Town Street. The displays in each room have been designed to reflect Dr. Hall's comparative wealth and status as the leading physician of Stratford. They also indicate that the family was devout in their religious faith. The docent pointed out the large oil painting in the parlor, the principal room of the house. This painting by Anthonius Claeissins (1538–1613) depicts a merchant and his family around the table saying grace before a meal. The docent reminded us that Dr. John Hall was also known for his strong religious faith and Puritan leanings.

As we made our way through this beautiful home, we could see that it had been well equipped as a doctor's office and a place for entertaining guests in an opulent style. On the second floor, there was a large laboratory room, and spacious bedrooms, as well as servants' quarters. The door from the back hall opens into a walled formal English garden. We walked down the long path to the sundial and arbor. From this vantage point, we had a fine view of the mansion with the flowers and gardens in the foreground.

The docent ended our tour of Hall's Croft by suggesting that Shakespeare's considerable medical knowledge almost certainly must have been derived from his close association with Dr. John Hall. She believed that Dr. Hall was William Shakespeare's personal physician and probably had attended him on his deathbed in 1616. When his father-in-law died, Dr. and Mrs. Hall moved from this location into New Place.[3]

When we left Hall's Croft, we headed to Holy Trinity Church. The church stands on the bank of the Avon River. The day was lovely and warm and somewhat overcast, and we enjoyed the park-like setting along the river. The white swans on the river added to the peaceful atmosphere of the church grounds. We were reminded of Francis Havergal's hymn: "Like a river glorious is God's perfect peace."

The church was built in classic Gothic style in the shape of a cross. This was the church where William Shakespeare and his family had worshipped. To us, the most important feature there is the grave of the famous playwright. He had been buried in the chancel in 1616. "This privilege was bestowed upon him as a 'lay rector,' which he became in 1605."[4] The inscription over his grave reads:

> Good friend for Jesus sake forbear
> To dig the dust enclosed here!
> Blest be the man that spares these stones
> And cursed be he that moves my bones.[5]

We also noted that his widow, Anne, and additional members of his family have been buried next to his tomb. On the north wall of the church, we found the bust of William Shakespeare, which, we were told, had been placed in the church about seven years following his death. His widow and many of his friends were still living when this was accomplished. The inscription below the bust reads:

> Iudicio Pylium, genio Socratem, arte Maronem:
> Terra tegit, populus maeret, Olympus habet.
>
> Stay passenger, why goest thou by so fast?
> Read if thou canst, whom Death enjoys hath past,
> Within this monument Shakespeare: with whom,
> Quick nature died: whose name doth deck the tomb,
> Far more than cost: see all, that he hath writ,
> Leaves living art, but page, to serve his wit.
> Obiit ano do 1616
> Aetatis 53 Die 23 Ap.[6]

I believe these inscriptions, along with the placing of his grave inside the church, are further proof that William Shakespeare was a devout Christian. I am constantly amazed to hear so many people claim that Shakespeare was an immoral man who could never have been a Christian.

Our time in Stratford did not allow us to take the trip out to the village of Wilmcote, where the home of the Arden family is located. However, here are some notations regarding this property that are important to this study. Mary Arden was the mother of William Shakespeare, and the daughter of Robert Arden. Robert died in 1556 and left his property to Mary, the youngest of eight daughters. "His bequest was probably made shortly in advance of her marriage to John Shakespeare."[7]

Since the Arden home was located in a small country community, it brings to mind the countryside setting of many of the bard's plays. Many of the sights and sounds of nature: wild flowers, birds and animals, farmers at work in the fields remind Shakespeare students of sections in his plays, such as the forest descriptions in *A Midsummer Night's Dream*. Another notation about the Arden farm is that it is located near the ancient tract of woodland from which the family name derived, the Forest of Arden. Shakespeare used this forest for the setting of his play, *As You Like It*. "The play's descriptive passages have a detailed, intimate quality that seems rooted in a personal knowledge of the dramatist's native countryside."[8]

From the Church of the Holy Trinity, we walked along the Avon River bank toward the center of town. We walked up Chapel Street to the site of New Place, the home Shakespeare had purchased for his family on May 4, 1597. The docent explained to us that, unfortunately, New Place had been torn down. After the surviving members of the Shakespeare family no longer lived in this house, it was sold to a man who did not like William Shakespeare. From time to time visitors would come to his door and ask for a tour of New Place. Finally, he became so angry that he ordered the entire house dismantled. The docent lamented the selfishness of this man who would rather have the the most important building in Stratford destroyed than to give it to the city for preservation.

On the site of New Place, a large formal English garden has been planted and preserved for the enjoyment of those visitors who come to Stratford to learn first-hand the facts about the great playwright. Actually, this large home originally stood on an acreage that included two gardens and two orchards. The site itself contains a special significance, because Shakespeare had owned this home, and he and his family lived there for nearly a third of William's life. It was in this building that he was thought to have written most of his plays. The Guild Chapel is located immediately to the south of the property, and the family would have viewed the Chapel from their garden.[9]

New Place had a distinguished history before William Shakespeare purchased it. It was the second largest home in Stratford, and the owners enjoyed a position of prestige and social standing in the community. The residents of this fine manor were also entitled to a special pew in the Holy Trinity Church, called the Clopton Pew. Sir Hugh Clopton, onetime Lord Mayor of London, had the house built in the 1500s. The Underhill family purchased the home when William was a boy living in his father's house on Henley Street. The house was badly in need of many repairs, so it is not surprising that Shakespeare bought New Place for only sixty pounds.[10]

Adjoining the property of New Place is another fine home, which had been purchased by Thomas Nash. He was a wealthy property-owner, who married Shakespeare's granddaughter, Elizabeth Hall in 1626. Elizabeth was the daughter of Dr. and Mrs. John Hall, who had moved to New Place shortly after William Shakespeare had died. Following the wedding of Thomas Nash to Elizabeth Hall, the newlyweds moved into the large mansion next door; for it was more than adequate for the two families. Other members of the Nash family continued to live in the old Nash house, which was left to Elizabeth when Thomas Nash died in 1647.[11]

The docent at Nash's House began her tour with an explanation of the loss of New Place: "It is most regretful that New Place has been demolished, but much of the history has been maintained in Nash's House." Because of their ownership by members of the Shakespeare family, both houses are linked together in history. The physical proximity of the two homes would have allowed the families to work closely together on various projects and community affairs. "At certain times throughout the history of these buildings," the docent explained, "what is now the Great Garden of New Place had belonged to the owners of Nash's House. But in other times, the residents of New Place had owned what is now part of Nash's gardens." It is these intertwined parts of the history of these two fine homes that make it appropriate today to use the site of Nash's House as an introduction to the history of New Place.

Of special note, we were told, is the second floor of Nash's House, which has not been furnished in an Elizabethan domestic style, but rather set up to house a museum detailing Stratford's long and varied history. One room has been set aside to house displays from Shakespeare's time and shows the visitor a room like the one where William Shakespeare would have written some of his plays. Another room is dedicated to the first Shakespeare festival, held in Stratford in 1769. The museum further documents the fact that the family of William Shakespeare, the playwright who was part owner of the drama company known as the King's Men in London, was a family who had played an important role in the history of Stratford-upon-Avon.

Our last stop was at the Shakespeare Visitor Center and Shakespeare's birthplace on Henley Street. The tour begins in the visitor center, where the exhibits feature the life of William Shakespeare, a scale model of the Globe Theatre, a first edition of his collected plays, and other items of interest, such as a desk from the Stratford grammar school.

The house on Henley Street is not only the birthplace of the playwright, but also the house where he was raised. He brought his bride to this home after they were married; it was customary in those days for the groom to bring his bride to his parents' home. The house is located in the center of town, and was an excellent site for John Shakespeare to work his leather craft. The docent told us that John Shakespeare was not only an expert in the art of making gloves, but he also had held some of the highest political offices in the town.

On the first floor of the Henley Street home is the large parlor. This room was used for entertaining guests and general day-time domestic purposes; it also probably served as a bedroom at night, since the Shakespeare family included several children and other relatives who lived with them. The furniture that has been placed in the house today has an interesting piece: an early seventeenth century armchair that had once been in the local village inn; but the most interesting feature of this room is its floor, whose broken slabs of stone are considered original from the time the house had been built.[12]

From the parlor there is a hall that leads to the workshop where Shakespeare's father is thought to have worked in his glove-making business. The evidence from the records in Stratford indicates that John Shakespeare had developed a thriving business in preparing, cutting, and sewing all kinds of leather, but his specialty was leather gloves. The workshop also included the store where the gloves and other leather items were sold, for he was also known as a "whittawer."[13]

The glovers were one of the most powerful trade groups in Stratford. On market days, the glovers set up booths in the center of town, under the big clock in the market square, where most of the merchants and local townspeople came to shop. It should also be noted that John Shakespeare was an enterprising businessman who dealt in other goods, such as timber and wool.[14]

The other major room on the first floor is the kitchen. This is a spacious area where the meals were both prepared and served around a large table. The family spent many hours together there, since it also served the purpose of our modern family room. The open hearth is equipped with cooking utensils, including a pair of iron stands to support the spits that were used for roasting meat and a large cooking-pot, which hangs over the fire. From the kitchen, a flight of stairs leads down to the cellar, where food supplies were stored.

The rooms upstairs are bedrooms, which are decorated to illustrate different aspects of Elizabethan era domestic life in households similar to the family home of the Shakespeares. The most notable room in the house is the one where, according to an early tradition, William was born. The docent explained to our group that even if this was not the exact room, it has been furnished appropriately. The display of furnishings has been carefully arranged to give a complete picture of how a birthroom would have appeared in Shakespeare's time.

The original furniture has been supplemented with replicas designed to show the authenticity of a room where a child would have been birthed. A textile-hung bed, painted cloths on the walls, and a "truckle-bed"[15] give visitors a birthroom atmosphere. We noted that some famous visitors, including Sir Walter Scott and Thomas Carlyle, scratched their names into the glass of the old latticed windows.

From our visit to Stratford, I drew several conclusions. We were able to learn first-hand many facts about the town where Shakespeare was born and raised, and details about his family background, culture, and social standing. We had the opportunity to experience the atmosphere of life in a small, prosperous town in Elizabethan times. The fact that Stratford was located on the Avon River, which was deep enough for small merchant ships to sail into port, explains how many businesses were able to prosper from international trade.

The visit to the Church, with Shakespeare's gravesite and testimony regarding his religious faith, enabled us to conclude that William Shakespeare was a devout Christian his entire life. The evidence in the homes where his family lived reinforced this belief. He was born into a family for whom the Christian religion was a vital part of their daily lives. His parents were raised in families of strong faith; he married a wife whose parents taught and followed the Bible in their everyday practice; both his daughters married men who were known to practice Scriptural principles.

Another conclusion I drew was that family life was of utmost importance to the members of the Shakespeare family. One of the greatest blessings a man such as William Shakespeare can enjoy is to be born into a multi-generational Christian home. Today in America we are seeing a slow destruction of the family because Christian values are no longer considered necessary for happiness. Even though Shakespeare did not grow up in a town where all the citizens were Christian, Stratford had a Christian environment. The morality of the Bible was expected of both Christians and non-Christians. London was not so blessed. Crime and corruption were frequent in this large city. But William Shakespeare wanted to raise his family in a different environment, one of peace and tranquillity, where God was honored in the community and in the home.

One last comment: with all the evidence throughout the town of Stratford, how could anyone possibly come to the conclusion that William Shakespeare never lived, or that some other person wrote his plays?

---

1 Roger Pringle, *The Shakespeare Houses: The Official Guide*, Norwich, England: Jarrold Publishing, in association with The Shakespeare Birthplace Trust, ISBN: 0711729492, 1998, 20–21.

2 Ibid., 16–19.

3 Ibid.

4 Pamphlet: "Holy Trinity Church, Stratford-upon-Avon," Section I. The Grave of William Shakespeare.

5 The spelling has been upgraded to more modern English.

6 The first section is in Latin, loosely translated: "In judgment, like Paul; in inclination to wisdom, like Socrates; in artistic skill, like Maro (a surname of Virgil); his land defends him; the people mourn him; Olympus has him." The last words, also in Latin, are translated: "He died in the year of our Lord, 1616, on April 23, at the age of 53."

7 Pringle, 26–27.

8 Ibid.

9 Ibid., 14.

10 Marchette Chute, *Shakespeare of London*, 1949, 186–187.

11 Pringle, 12.

12 Chute, 1949, 7.

13 *Whittawer*: a dealer in the fine white leather from which the best products were made.

14 Chute, 1949, 2.

15 *truckle-bed*: trundle bed.

Chapter Eight

"I Am Constant as the Northern Star"

Character Development

*J*ULIUS CAESAR proclaims shortly before his assassination: "I am constant as the northern star, of whose true-fixed and resting quality, there is no fellow in the firmament."[1] In the context of the play, *Julius Caesar,* we learn several things about Caesar's character. He considers himself invincible; he misjudges the conspirators; his overblown ego will not allow him to sense the danger around him. This, of course, is the character which William Shakespeare derived from historical documents as well as what scholars had said about Julius Caesar. But, more importantly, it is the character that Shakespeare molded into his own presentation of the man Julius Caesar, whose brilliant strategies in war and politics had carried him into the position of Roman emperor.

The use of character development is a key factor in writing drama. Shakespeare sharpened this skill throughout his writing career, and he achieved this by showing in the characters of his plays their detailed personality traits intertwined with their moral character in such a way that audiences often identify with some of his characters. This identification may be one of like or dislike, trust or distrust, and in some cases, love or hate. Hamlet, Lear, Richard II, Dogberry, Falstaff are merely characters in a play, but they become so alive on the stage that they seem nearly real to the serious Shakespeare student. Often, when a play is well presented, members of the audience will develop intense feelings toward one or more of its characters.

Noah Webster defines *character* as: "A mark made by cutting or engraving, as on a stone, metal or other hard material; hence a mark or figure made with a pen or style, on paper, or other material used to contain writing; a letter, or figure used to form words, and communicate ideas."[2] When we start with this definition, we are reminded of what God did when he formed Adam.[3] The Bible says: "And the Lord God formed man of the dust of the ground, and breathed into his nostrils the breath of life, and man became a living soul."[4] Here we have the concept that God created man in His own image. In other words, God took the clay and engraved His own character into His created being.

In Genesis, chapter one, God said: "Let us make man in our own image, after our likeness: and let them have dominion over the fish of the sea, and over the fowl of the air, and over the cattle, and over all the earth, and over every creeping thing that creepeth upon the earth."[5] The dominion command by God to Adam (man) reveals some important factors in man's inborn character. Man, by his created nature, wants to own land and be the master over it. Man, by nature, yearns to be free to follow the dictates of his own conscience. Man sees his life as important because God gave him dominion over his own property. William Shakespeare was educated in a school that taught these principles; therefore, he naturally would have applied some of these basic God-given traits to the characters he invented through his art.

Going on to another definition from Noah Webster, we read: *character* is "the peculiar qualities, impressed by nature or habit on a person, which distinguish him from others; these constitute real character, and the qualities which he is supposed to possess, constitute his estimated character, or reputation. Hence we say, a character is not formed, when the person has not acquired stable and distinctive qualities."[6] William Shakespeare was a genius in this aspect of describing the peculiar qualities of each of his characters and making them come alive on the stage. Shakespeare created in the plot and dialogue degrees of character formation that enabled the audience to see the change in each character as the play progressed.

Shakespeare for Everyone to Enjoy

Because Shakespeare often developed the theme of evil and its consequences, it may be concluded that he drew his basic understanding of evil and sin from the Bible. God created man in His own image and said that this was very good. But God also gave Adam total free will. That is, Adam was free to obey God's commands or to follow his own desires. Since God had commanded Adam not to eat of the Tree of the Knowledge of Good and Evil, Adam was free to obey or disobey. When Satan, in the form of the serpent, tempted Eve to eat the fruit of this forbidden tree, she not only ate, but also gave some to her husband, and he ate.[7]

At this point, sin and evil entered into God's created universe. Because all men are born with Adam's sin nature, Paul states in his letter to the Romans: "For all have sinned, and come short of the glory of God."[8] As I gave evidence in chapter four concerning Shakespeare's religion, he followed the traditional Biblical view establishing the cause of sin. For the same reason, Shakespeare saw that man could be redeemed by the power of Jesus Christ in his death on the cross and resurrection from the grave. Although Shakespeare never stated the theological details concerning man's conversion in his plays, he assumed that his audiences were familiar with the Biblical details of theology. Shakespeare wrote one play that demonstrates these principles: *As You Like It*. The title of the play suggests that those in the audience may view the play any way they please, that is, with or without the theological inferences.

In *As You Like It*, the Forest of Arden becomes a tool for character development. Everyone who goes into the Forest is affected by some kind of "magical power," which brings about changes in his personality and character. Duke Frederick has banished his brother, Duke Senior, from his own kingdom. When we meet Duke Senior in the play, living in the Forest of Arden, he has become a wiser man. But no one is affected as much as Duke Frederick. Frederick's whole life is turned around, so that he forsakes his evil and vengeful deeds, which had brought him his position of power. When Duke Frederick went to the Forest of Arden, his desire was to punish those who had rebelled against his authority. Much to his surprise, he encounters a man of "religious" character. Instead of continuing in his evil ways, he is converted so that he becomes a new creature whose desire is to restore to the rightful owner the lands he had taken by force.[9]

Another evil man, Oliver de Boys, the eldest son of Sir Roland de Boys, is also converted when he goes to the Forest. Duke Frederick has sent Oliver to find his brother Orlando, the youngest son of Sir Roland, to bring him back dead or alive. The duke is incensed, so his purpose is to punish. Orlando's clever wit and physical strength keep him from being killed through the duke's subversive plans. Oliver also wished for his brother's death. Orlando had wandered into the Forest of Arden after he had become restless under the neglect and contempt that Oliver showed him. When a lion ferociously attacks Oliver, Orlando saves his life. At this point in the play, Oliver is no longer seen to be the cruel and overbearing brother, intent on doing evil. Miraculously, he has been changed into a forgiving and loving brother, who finds his true love in the banished Duke Senior's daughter, Celia.

Shakespeare used the role of the fool in several of his plays to help change the character of others. I have previously mentioned how the Fool in *King Lear* led the king through his times of suffering so that Lear emerged a wiser man. It is possible that Shakespeare may have been inspired to develop the character of some of his "fools" by Paul's letter to the Corinthian church. Paul wrote to the Corinthians: "For God hath chosen the foolish things of the world to confound the wise; and God hath chosen the weak things of the world to confound the mighty."[10] It is the fool who brings to his master and others in the play the wisdom to see through their darkness, which they previously considered wisdom. The character of the fool often has a servant role, or has been assigned a role which is inferior to those with whom he is dialoguing.

The role of the comic fool is found in some of Shakespeare's most effective comedies. One of my favorite fools is Dogberry in *Much Ado about Nothing*. Dogberry is the bumbling police officer, accompanied by an entire group of volunteer policemen, who, it would appear, can do nothing right. However, amazingly, they do catch the crooks! In the process, Dogberry and company solve the mystery that surrounds the maligned Hero, whose fiancé, Claudio, has refused to marry her because of her reputed immorality. Dogberry supplies the wisdom, revealing that Claudio and Hero are the victims of a vengeful plot by the wicked Don John. In the following speech, Dogberry displays both his inability to say things correctly as well as his enjoyment in being the fool:

> Dost thou not suspect[11] my place? Dost thou not suspect my years? Oh, that he were here to write me down an ass! But, masters, remember that I am an ass, though it be not written down, yet forget not that I am an ass. No, thou villain, thou art full of piety,[12] as shall be proved upon thee by good witness. I am a wise fellow, and, which is more, an officer; and, which is more, a householder; and, which is more, as pretty a piece of flesh as any in Messina; and one that knows the law, go to; and a rich fellow enough, go to; and a fellow that hath had losses; and one that hath two gowns, and everything handsome about him. Bring him away. Oh, that I had been writ down an ass![13]

The greatest and most beloved of all Shakespeare's fools is Sir John Falstaff. A different type of fool, he was a villain who is the butt of others' jokes. His character is such that he appealed to both the intellectuals and the groundlings. The fat knight is depicted as a fallen man, who though he achieved a university education, chose to carouse with thieves and prostitutes. Falstaff's appetites are out of control, since he decided to forget the disciplines he had learned, so that he can enjoy his sensuous living. Shakespeare spends the length of three plays to develop his character, which comes to a tragic end when his pal, the wayward prince Hal, becomes the king. One of Falstaff's most moving lines is when he meets an old college friend, Justice Shallow. While they are reminiscing over past experiences, Falstaff says: "We have heard the chimes at midnight, Master Shallow."[14]

Falstaff had gained such popularity with the Elizabethan audiences that they clamored for one more play about Falstaff. In *The Merry Wives of Windsor*, Shakespeare depicts Falstaff as a fool who thinks he can outwit the foolish husbands of the merry wives, but it is the merry wives who outwit him. This is the only play that Shakespeare wrote with a domestic setting, and with characters that are ordinary middle-class people. The setting in the town of Windsor is perfect for such a delightfully funny tale. Two cheerful women get the best of the London knight in a series of mishaps that keep the audience in stitches. Marchette Chute sums the play up by stating: "The play is a long, lively game in which they (the wives) are the delightful victors."[15]

The development of comic character is a superb mark of William Shakespeare's works, but the Bard showed even greater mastery in developing the strengths and weaknesses of those characters who must strive against the tides of immorality. In some cases, such characters master their weaknesses, but in others, they fail to use their inner strength to overcome the external powers working to destroy them. The internal character or conscience must overcome the external forces or succumb to them; it is this internal-external conflict that Shakespeare used to drive his plot development, which will mark the final end of each character.

The method Shakespeare employed for character development in his plays is reflective of man's natural, God-given process for maturing his character. This is also the same pattern a Christian follows to become the Christian God has designed him to be. If we follow our *internal* commands, based on God's Word, we will find *external* results pleasing to God. James Rose points out how the *internal* gives rise to the *external* with a chart on character showing the *internal* as the cause and the *external* as the effect:

INTERNAL (causative—a conflict within)

"Seeks to honestly, conscientiously examine and prove (try, test) himself by the Word of God"

(II Corinthians 13:5, I Timothy 3:16–17)

EXTERNAL (effect—a conflict without)

"Perceives and corrects errors in his own conduct as a citizen even when both friends and public officials praise his conduct [before it has been corrected.]"[16]

This chart demonstrates the internal struggle a Christian must endure before he takes an external stand in society. This is also true of men who choose evil. If the internal forces put into a man's mind an immoral image, he will face a greater conflict to externally act according to that force. Macbeth provides a good example. The witches put into his mind the concept that he would become the Thane of Cawdor, with the possibility of also becoming King. With this concept internalized, Macbeth writes a letter containing these predictions to his wife. Lady Macbeth internalizes this promising future and begins to plot how to bring it about. The resulting external actions are a series of murders.

The tragic figures in Shakespeare's plays generally deteriorate from good to evil or from bad to worse. This is especially marked in the characters of Othello, Timon of Athens, Antony, Cleopatra, Troilus, and Richard III. Others learn their lessons, but not in time to stop God's predestined judgment: Hamlet, the Capulet and Montague parents, Lear, and Richard II.

Because this pattern of moving from internal thought to external action is basic to all men, we identify Shakespeare's characters as realistic. This is not to say that other playwrights do not follow the same pattern. What I am pointing to is that Shakespeare was more adept at character development than most other writers. Furthermore, his middle and later plays demonstrate increased skill in this ability than his earlier ones.

The first play Shakespeare wrote that shows great depth in the character development from the beginning to the end of the play is Richard II. Harrison states: "The play is the drama of the failure and death of a King, but Richard's tragedy is not that he came to degradation, misery, and death, but that he wrought his own destruction."[17] When the play opens, Richard is seen as a man of great charm, who is weak, selfish, and unscrupulous. He is also too easily attracted to his own reflection. He must always be the center of attention, no matter how important the part of another character may be in a given situation.

In the first scene of the play, Richard takes the position of a stern judge, who says: "We were not born to sue but to command."[18] Richard has ordered the Duke of Norfolk and Henry Bolingbroke to fight a duel to settle their differences; however, after they have assembled at the lists of

Coventry, he suddenly stops the fight and attracts attention away from the combatants to himself. He announces the harsh sentence of exile on them both. This is a particularly painful sentence for Bolingbroke. Not only is he Richard's cousin, but he also loves England and is loved and respected by many Englishmen. This act will cause much grief for Richard's future; for Bolingbroke believes he has a valid claim to the throne.

As the play progresses, the audience observes how the internal forces of Richard's character force his external actions almost to the point of what we might call fate ("predestination," for the theologian). When he takes command of a military expedition to Ireland, he envisions himself as the soldier king. But when he goes to the bedside of the dying John of Gaunt, he is mean-spirited and impertinent. Richard will not hear the truthful cautions of a dying man, who should have been given great respect. The internal attitude of self-importance brought condemnation for Richard's actions of disrespect from John of Gaunt: "And thy unkindness be like crooked age, to crop at once a too-long-withered flower, live in thy shame, but die not shame with thee!"[19]

A rebellion breaks out in England under the leadership of Bolingbroke, but King Richard is convinced that Heaven would never permit an anointed king to lose his power and position. There was a doctrine held in Elizabethan days that all kings were chosen by God, and that only God can remove a king who has failed to reign with righteousness. Again Richard stood on his inner convictions, and failed to gain the wisdom to understand the danger that lay at his doorstep. If only he had listened to John of Gaunt's wisdom! It was too late. The kingdom was crumbling, with desertion all around his throne. Then Richard was friendless and powerless, ranting and raving against his enemies, believing that God would send His angels to save him and his tottering throne.

Even in defeat, Richard took a morbid delight in turning his kingdom over to the usurper Bolingbroke:

> I'll give my jewels for a set of beads,
> My gorgeous palace for a hermitage,
> My gay apparel for an almsman's gown,

My figured goblets for a dish of wood,
My scepter for a palmer's walking-staff,
My subjects for a pair of carved saints,
And my large kingdom for a little grave,
A little grave, an obscure grave. . . .[20]

In a later speech, Richard declared: "With mine own hands I give away my crown."[21] Henry Bolingbroke was not content just to receive the crown from Richard, but he insisted that Richard make a full confession of his crimes. This leads to the famous looking-glass scene, where Richard showed contempt for those who tried to force him to sign a false confession. Richard is lost in his own self-pity:

Thou dost beguile me! Was this face the face
That every day under his household roof
Did keep ten thousand men? Was this the face
That, like the sun, did make beholders wink?
Was this the face that faced so many follies,
And was at last outfaced by Bolingbroke?
A brittle glory shineth in this face—
As brittle as the glory is the face.
[Dashes the glass against the ground.]
For there it is, cracked in a hundred shivers.
Mark, silent King, the moral of this sport,
How soon my sorrow hath destroyed my face.[22]

As King Henry went to London to be crowned the new king, Richard was sent to prison in Pomfret Castle. Here we have a deposed and saddened Richard, who is now contemplating the meaning of the entire sordid experience. Richard considers the events that brought about his downfall, and repents his failure to be a good, gracious, and strong king. He sums up his estate with these prophetic words: "I wasted time, and now doth time waste me."[23] After Richard made his confession, Exton and two armed men entered his prison cell. In the fight, Richard valiantly killed the two men, but, then, Exton struck him down. As Richard died, he prophesied that the whole land would be stained with his blood.[24]

We will always be indebted to William Shakespeare for his wonderful portrayals of the many and varied characters in his plays. I recommend seeing each play several times, since every director adds his own touch, causing the viewer to grasp more of the depth of each play as it comes to the stage. This is true of artistic director Libbey Appel, whose personal oversight of the directors and each cast and her personal concern for the patrons has continued to offer so many fine performances year after year, bringing the Oregon Shakespeare Festival to a new level of excellence.

---

1 *Julius Caesar*, Act III, scene 1, lines 60–62.

2 Noah Webster, *An American Dictionary of the English Language*, 1828 Facsimile Edition; reprint San Francisco: Foundation for American Christian Education, 1967 & subsequent editions from Chesapeake, VA, "character," definition 1. a.

3 The Hebrew word "adam" is translated "man, mankind"; cf. Brown, Driver, Briggs: *A Hebrew and English Lexicon of the Old Testament*, London: Oxford U. Press, 1907, 9.

4 Genesis 2:7, KJV.

5 Genesis 1:26, KJV.

6 Webster, "character," definition 4.

7 Genesis 2:16–3:7.

8 Romans 3:23, KJV.

9 Marchette Chute, *Stories from Shakespeare*, NY: World Publishing Co., 1956, 81.

10 I Corinthians 1:27, KJV.

11 *suspect*: Dogberry actually means *respect*.

12 *piety*: actually means *impiety*.

13 *Much Ado about Nothing*, Act IV, scene 2, lines 76–90.

14 *Henry IV*, Part II, Act III, scene 2, line 238.

15 Chute, 1956, 67.

16 James B. Rose, *A Guide to American Christian Education for the Home and School*, Palo Cedro, CA: American Christian History Institute, 1987, 40; (bracketed words are mine).

17 G. B. Harrison, ed., *Shakespeare, Major Plays*, 192.

18 *Richard II*, Act I, scene 1, line 196.

19 Ibid., Act II, scene 1, lines 133–135.

20 Ibid., Act III, scene 3, lines 147–154.

21 Ibid., Act IV, scene 1, line 208.

22 Ibid., Act IV, scene 1, lines 281–291; *shivers*: meaning, "splinters."

23 Ibid., Act V, scene 5, line 49.

24 Chute, 1956, 272.

Chapter Nine

"The Play's the Thing"

Shakespeare in the Classroom

MY fondest remembrances of Shakespeare classes were at the University of Southern California, when Dr. Frank Baxter was reading from the plays and relating the impact that he had gained from Shakespeare over the years. Dr. Baxter taught by reading aloud the most important sections of each play with such feeling that we were mesmerized. This was a class where I never saw a student dozing or preoccupied with another subject. Dr. Baxter had a certain depth of understanding as well as a profound ability to read the plays with such precise meaning that we hung on every word.

"The play's the thing wherein I'll catch the conscience of the king."[1] That was a line we would never forget, because we could be sure it would appear on one of Dr. Baxter's exams. But more important, it was a key line in Hamlet's character progression. We were taught that key lines were the means to understanding the play in depth. *Hamlet* is one of Shakespeare's most moving plays, and it is my favorite.

Another of Shakespeare's best plays is *Henry V.* When Dr. Baxter lectured on this play, he had already taken us through *Richard II, Henry IV,* Part I, and *Henry IV,* Part II. Frank Baxter had learned the importance of working through these four plays in order, because they are based on history, which begins with the reign of Richard II and ends with that of Henry V. William Shakespeare drew his historical information from Raphael Holinshed's *Chronicles of England, Scotland, and Ireland*, published in 1577, and reissued in a second edition in 1587.[2] The bard followed the historical chronology and drew his characters from the *Chronicles*, but he added his own character development to fit the movement of each play.

Dr. Baxter emphasized the fact that the history plays and their characters do not necessarily follow the constraints of historical fact, but that they were embellished with Shakespeare's own artistic devices. For example, Richard II probably was not a theatrical personage as portrayed in the play; Shakespeare took Richard's weak character and painted him as a king who gave away his crown to Henry Bolingbroke in a moment of dramatic and poetic display. History does not record whether Henry IV was deeply concerned about the dangers he had placed upon England because he had stolen the crown from Richard; however, Shakespeare makes this an important factor in his presentation of the character of Henry IV.

Another important lesson we learned from Frank Baxter was that Shakespeare added characters, such as Falstaff, Pistol, and Mistress Quickly, to bring humor to what could have been a dull history play. Also, we learned that Shakespeare had used these characters as the setting in which the audience becomes acquainted with Prince Hal in his wild days of growing up. By the time we were ready to study *Henry V,* Dr. Baxter had already given us a thorough study of the preceding plays. It is important to know this background in order to understand the reign of Henry V, one of England's greatest kings.

Angus Bowmer told me once that he always rotated the history plays each year at Ashland, so that every ten years, audiences could go through the entire history canon chronologically from King John to Henry VIII. I had the pleasure of seeing each play in rotation during the 1960s and 1970s. Unfortunately, the program of the Oregon Shakespeare Festival in Ashland no longer presents the history plays in rotation. Seeing all ten plays in rotation could help other history buffs like me gain a valuable perspective of English history difficult to attain by just reading books. Certainly Shakespeare's dramatizations provide more enjoyment of history than books alone. Perhaps the leadership of the Oregon Shakespeare Festival will someday want to consider another ten-year rotation for the history plays.

Both Frank Baxter and Angus Bowmer believed in the importance of studying the history plays in order. *Henry V* is such a wonderful play on its own, but the study of the three previous plays assists the student in finding a richer, deeper understanding into the character of Henry V, and the problems he faced during his reign. Besides this, there is also a continuing development of Falstaff and his friends that carries over into *Henry V.* Therefore, I recommend this approach for any serious student of Shakespeare.

To illustrate this point, Dr. Baxter carefully took his students through the problem of usurping the power of the throne. Richard believed that he could not be removed from power, because God had put him on the throne of England. God would surely bring judgment upon anyone who would try to remove a divinely anointed king. After Henry had usurped the throne, Shakespeare depicts him as deeply concerned that God would not only bring His judgment on him, but on England as well. When we move on into the three parts of *Henry VI,* we will see Shakespeare raising this issue as England is thrown into civil war. Is the War of the Roses God's judgment for Henry Bolingbroke's sin?

While studying *Henry IV,* Parts I and II, we learn about the character of Prince Hal. He is associating with a group of wayward and dissolute companions, including that most wonderful fellow, Sir John Falstaff. This association alone would have been enough to give Hal's father a few gray hairs. Falstaff, the fat knight, is completely outrageous, a coward, a thief, and a drunkard. In spite of all these negatives, he is also completely irresistible. Marchette Chute describes Falstaff in the following manner. "He is so buoyantly charmed by being alive, so delighted with himself and his own disgraceful activities, and such a magnificent realist in a world given to self-deception, that he sweeps through what might have been an orderly play of noble deeds and thoughts and turns everything upside down without even caring. He may be a bad influence on Prince Hal, but he is a wonderful influence on the play."[3]

Falstaff moves about among rogues, prostitutes, and thieves. Among his friends are Mistress Quickly, Poins, Bardolph, Pistol, and Doll Tearsheet, all of which were greatly enjoyed by the groundlings. In this setting, Prince Hal seems to be rebelling against his future role as king, and there is some concern that he may not have the character required to rule England well. When the play, *Henry IV*, closes, Shakespeare depicts Prince Hal as a reformed, serious young prince who is ready to take on the responsibilities required of the King of England. Sir John Falstaff, however, is not ready to be reformed, for he still expects his dear friend, now the King, to offer him an important position in his new government. But he is sadly mistaken and is sent to prison instead.

G. B. Harrison, when discussing the nature of the history play, said: "A history play, Shakespeare claimed, did not attempt to be realistic; its aim was rather to stimulate the imagination of the spectator."[4] Dr. Baxter, who used Harrison's book for a text, agreed. The invention of characters such as Falstaff and Mistress Quickly allowed the members of the audience to imagine the relationship of the common people of England to the nobility, who were the actual rulers of the land. Not only did this technique show the importance of the common folk within the entire picture of daily life in England, it also drew the common man of Shakespeare's day into the theater. England had a history that demonstrated the importance of every man, whether he was born to aristocracy or not.

The focus of the Magna Charta was on the common man, his rights and liberties, and that the king was subject to the same laws as every other citizen. This great historical document formed the foundation of English common law. Samuel Adams said in the *Boston Gazette*, on January 9, 1769: ". . . as long as the people understand the great charter of nature upon which Magna Charta itself is founded, no man can take another's property from him without his consent. This is the law of nature; and a violation of it is the same thing, whether it be done by one man who is called a king, or by five hundred of another denomination. . . ."[5] William Shakespeare could be considered a champion for the common man, except that he showed the same concern for the nobility. That was part of his genius—an understanding of the plight of men in all stations of life.

Therefore, we are not surprised to find a special emphasis upon Falstaff and his friends in a historical play. When *Henry V* opens, England has been thrown into war with France, and Henry must lead his soldiers into a battle where the French troops vastly outnumber the English. Dr. Baxter could stir up the bravest hearts when he read that great speech Henry delivered as he prepared his men for battle: "Once more unto the breach, dear friends, once more. . . ."[6] We now know that King Henry had been well prepared for his position in history. He is not only a strong king, but he is a leader of men. Perhaps even he had learned about life, especially the common man, when he had been carousing with Falstaff and his friends. Perhaps his life as a seemingly rebellious prince had helped to build the character he would need as a successful ruler. Although the play never directly states these ideas, they are assumed.

Dr. Baxter believed that Shakespeare considered Henry V to be one of England's greatest kings. This is quite evident throughout the study of the play. In the first part of the play, we see that Henry had learned how to execute justice when he sentenced those who were guilty of treason to death, but he also gave them an opportunity to repent before the death penalty was inflicted so they might not go to Hell.[7]

Meanwhile, the boy who has been a servant to Falstaff summons Hostess Quickly (who is now married to Pistol) to Falstaff's deathbed. The character of the boy is of special interest. He seems to have been an orphan, who survives by serving those whose reputations are suspect. When Hostess Quickly attends to the dying Falstaff, she is convinced that he has gone to heaven. Her famous lines describe his death: "Nay, sure, he's not in hell; he's in Arthur's bosom,[8] if ever a man went to Arthur's bosom."[9] However, the boy seems to question her belief because he is troubled about Falstaff's relationship with women. When Bardolph raises the question of "women," the hostess denies this, but the boy states: "Yes, that 'a did, and said they (women) were devils incarnate."[10] The logical conclusion is that the boy was convinced that Falstaff had never repented his evil ways, and must have gone to Hell.

When the call to service in France is made, Bardolph, Pistol, Nym, and the boy sign up with the army to fight in France. In a marvelous soliloquy, the boy shows that his character has surpassed that of the three older men.

> As young as I am, I have observed these three swashers. I am boy to all three of them. But all they three, though they would serve me, could not be man to me, for indeed three such "antics"[11] do not amount to a man . . . [The boy continues to list the sins of Bardolph, Pistol, and Nym. They are all filthy-mouthed thieves, who want him to help them steal and pillage the spoils of war.]. . . . Which makes much against my manhood, if I should take from another's pockets to put into mine, for it is plain pocketing-up of wrongs. I must leave them, and seek some better service. Their villainy goes against my weak stomach, and therefore, I must cast it up."[12]

Later the boy has joined the other boys who watch over the equipment and supplies. During this time, the French soldiers attack the unarmed boys, killing them all.

The Chorus prepares the audience for the great battle of Agincourt, telling how the King disguises himself as a soldier, going from camp to camp, encouraging his men, who have great fear because the French outnumber the English. Dr. Baxter would pause as he read one of his favorite lines from the Chorus, which beautifully describes the coming scenes: "A little touch of Harry in the night."[13]

Frank Baxter worked out his teaching method from his own experiences with Shakespeare's works. By the time I arrived at USC, he had become a legend at the university, and his classes filled rapidly at the time of registration. Because his classes were adapted for a large number of students, there was little opportunity for discussion in the classroom. His style of lecture was particularly suited to a large classroom. In addition to his reading from the plays, he allowed about a third of his lecture time to describe Elizabethan England, Shakespeare's family life, Stratford, London, the Elizabethan theater, and the success of Shakespeare's work.

Dr. Baxter did not allow much class time for a discussion of Shakespeare's sonnets, but he did require us to read about ten of them, which he discussed very briefly. He thought the sonnets to be of little value for determining facts about Shakespeare, and he was suspect of those scholars that attempted to derive information about Shakespeare's life and character from a study of his sonnets. One thing that impressed me was Dr. Baxter's model, which he had built, of the Globe Theatre. By looking at this model of the Globe, I could imagine the actors on the Elizabethan stage, while Dr. Baxter would read through parts of a play. What became clear was the fact that an actor had to project the meaning of the play with his voice and actions. Shakespeare usually put his players on a bare stage, with few sound effects, and no lighting on the outdoor stage. We have been accustomed to having elaborate scenery and special effects in most of our theaters today.

My method of teaching Shakespeare's plays has evolved from a different perspective. Most of my classes have been relatively small, and this allows for a great deal more discussion. When I was teaching at Chabot College in Hayward, California, my classes tended to range between twenty and thirty students. Also, I discovered that I could assist the students by stimulating them to ask questions. One of my supervisors visited a class I was teaching and observed that the atmosphere was somewhat stilted. She suggested that we arrange our chairs in a circle, so that all the students would feel more relaxed and free to ask questions. I adapted this procedure for teaching adults, but later I discovered that it did not work as well at the elementary and high school levels.

After I began experimenting with teaching the plays by having the students sit in a circle, I noticed that they had a desire to participate in the reading of the play. At first, I assigned the various roles about a week before we would read through a play, so that they would feel more comfortable, having had preparation time. Before long, I found the students willing to read from sight. I began each play with an introduction concerning the theme and the spiritual principles they should look for. After we had read a few scenes, I would question them on the character development.

I did not follow Dr. Baxter's method of working through the plays chronologically. What I had realized in my early years of teaching was that most of my students signed up for my classes because they knew nothing about Shakespeare and his plays and wanted to learn more. Most of Dr. Baxter's students already knew something about the Bard and his plays. My students were usually taking a required course, and I would need to make Shakespeare enjoyable for them. Therefore, I always started with one of the comedies that was easy to understand and which would quickly grab the imagination of the student.

This is an excellent place to begin in a homeschool situation. Begin with one of the lighter comedies, such as *The Comedy of Errors*, *A Midsummer Night's Dream*, *The Taming of the Shrew*, or *The Merry Wives of Windsor*. Once the student is hooked on Shakespeare, he will want more. Then you can move on to *Julius Caesar*, *Richard III*, or *As You Like It*. Usually, after two or three of the lighter plays, the students are ready for the heavy tragedies. I always start with *Macbeth*. Then I might teach *Richard II* or *The Tempest*. After the student has become familiar with four or five plays, I would teach *King Lear* or *Hamlet*.

I would make a recommendation for homeschool students to study Shakespeare: form a group of students from other families who homeschool. Read through one of the plays together. Find a book that comments on that particular play, and discuss the contents with the group. If the play is being performed in your area, take your group to a live performance. If a stage performance is not available, get a video copy from the library and view it together as a group. Always discuss the play again after the group has seen the play. In this way, students who do not attend a formal school, whether the school is private or government-sponsored, will have an opportunity to learn from each other's experiences.

Many of my lectures have been in connection with the Oregon Shakespeare Festival at Ashland. For these classes, I am constricted to the schedule of the season. But the advantage here is that the students are going to see the plays, usually so well done that evaluation time is the highlight of the schedule. Even when a play is not presented to my standards of perfection, the discussions are lively, because there is much to be learned from misinterpretations of both plot and characters. In some cases, most of the characters are well cast, but one or two may be miscast.

Shakespeare for Everyone to Enjoy

Most of my students who return almost every season have discovered how to spot errors in casting or problems in the plot. The best atmosphere for learning to enjoy Shakespeare is to have available plays that are well done. However, a lack of the best atmosphere should never deter anyone from trying to gain a better understanding of Shakespeare's plays.

What about students who attend private or public schools that do not offer classes in Shakespeare? Unfortunately, Shakespeare is not regularly taught in many schools today. Even some colleges no longer offer classes in the classics. My suggestion for those students who want to study the works of Shakespeare when it is not offered in the school curriculum: form a group and petition the faculty to add Shakespeare to the curriculum. Some of the young people that have attended our lecture series in Ashland have done just that. And they were successful.

Since my teaching methods have been almost entirely molded by the Ashland seminars, the only thing we do not do in the Ashland study group is read the plays out loud. All students are asked to read the plays before they come to the conference. Because the group sees the plays acted on the stage as an integral part of the conference, it is not necessary to read the plays together.

In some Shakespeare classes, entire plays are not studied, but only parts of a select number of plays. I do not recommend this approach. It is much better to study one entire play than to take sections from several plays. I make this notation because I have drawn from various plays throughout this book, with the purpose of making particular emphases on different aspects of Shakespeare's work. What I shall do now is give a brief overview of one play to give the student a concept for teaching one play.

At the beginning of this chapter, I quoted from *Hamlet*, the last line of one of his soliloquies. Although there is not enough space here for a detailed study of the entire play, I will outline the most important points. The nature of the play was a well-known type of drama, called the "revenge" play. Most revenge plays were written in a common scheme whereby the duty of vengeance following a crime, usually murder, was laid on the next of kin. The plot took on a pattern, where the discovery of the crime was followed by a presentation of the difficulties in bringing about revenge, and concluded with the triumphal killing of the murderer.[14]

In *Hamlet*, the revenge aspect involves the murder of Hamlet's father by his brother, Claudius. Not only has Claudius murdered his own brother, but also he has carried out an adulterous affair with Hamlet's mother, Gertrude. Following the death of the King, Claudius and Gertrude are married. All these events have occurred while Hamlet is away at college. Therefore, the responsibility of avenging his father's death lies with Hamlet, who has become the rightful king, although Claudius has usurped the throne and assumed the right to be king. Hamlet's responsibility is, first, to discover the murderer, and then to take his inherited position as the King of Denmark.

Although Shakespeare wrote this play in the revenge mode, the actual theme of *Hamlet* is the tragedy of indecision.[15] Sometimes scholars have called this play a drama of doubt, but I do not find doubt to be the major focus of the play. Rather it is a tragedy of a good man who cannot make a decision until it is too late. Procrastination is Hamlet's greatest weakness. In this play, it is deadly. One of the reasons I find this play so engrossing is that I find it easy to identify with Hamlet. I have had my own difficulties in dealing with my desires to procrastinate, to put off an important decision, or sometimes to allow myself to put off little things that I do not enjoy doing. In this way, I have identified with Hamlet, although my situation has never been as serious as that of Hamlet.

The most serious matters in life often involve details that need proof before they can be carried out, and we must have a plan to initiate action before we can move forward. We often need good counsel and a time of meditation to be sure we are doing the right thing. Other times, action must be done quickly. Hamlet is caught in this web of confusion, most of which is his own making. Even when he gets confirmation, he is incapable of carrying out his plan. Shakespeare shows us then how much greater the tragedy becomes. At several points in the play, if Hamlet had acted quickly, tragedy could have been avoided.

Shakespeare uses the device of the soliloquy to tell the audience about Hamlet's character development. There are eight soliloquies in all. In each of these speeches delivered to the audience, Hamlet reveals more about his character and the difficulties he is experiencing because of his inability to move from indecision to action. This is the only play in which Shakespeare used the soliloquy to frame the movement of the drama, so that the audience becomes the primary recipient of Hamlet's inner thoughts. Dr. Baxter defined the soliloquy as the actor speaking to himself; however, for the sake of the development of the plot, the primary recipient of his thoughts is the audience.

Shakespeare was adept in finding names for his characters and places that served a purpose related to his plots. In *Measure for Measure*, he invented Elbow, Froth, and Mistress Overdone. Names such as Bottom, Flute, Snout, Starveling, Moth, Cobweb, and Mustardseed appear in *A Midsummer Night's Dream*. Falstaff has friends named Doll Tearsheet, Justice Shallow, Pistol, and Fang and Snare are sheriff's officers. The setting for *As You Like It* takes place in the Forest of Arden, the forest named after the Arden family (Shakespeare's mother).

Hamlet was the name of a Danish prince in pre-Christian times, and there were several stories and plays in Elizabethan times about Hamlet. Especially significant is the French story told in *Histoires Tragiques*, written by Francois de Belleforest. Shakespeare followed the Belleforest plot line to some degree, but invents most of the details for his own play. Although Shakespeare did not invent the name of Hamlet or the simple story line, I believe he may have chosen this name for the play in which he philosophizes about his own inner thoughts and beliefs. *Hamlet* was written sometime just before 1600 or 1601. On August 11, 1596, the church records at Stratford-upon-Avon state that Hamnet, Shakespeare's only son, was buried. Is it possible that his father read the story of Hamlet and decided to write a play entitled *Hamlet* because of the similarity in the two names? If this were true, then the deep philosophical and theological questions raised in the play, especially through the soliloquies, would indicate that Hamnet's death had a profound effect upon Shakespeare's thinking and writing.

The bare outline of the story of the play will assist our discussion. The play opens on a cold, dark winter night in Denmark during the watch on the battlements of the castle. A ghost, in appearance like the late King of Denmark, becomes visible to the officer in charge, who then summons Horatio, Hamlet's school friend, to view the ghost. Horatio and the officer decide to find Hamlet to see if the Ghost will speak to him. Hamlet is at this point learning some dreadful news, that his mother with indecent haste has married his uncle, who has supplanted Hamlet, the rightful heir. Horatio convinces Hamlet to go up to the battlements and find out what the Ghost wants to say. Hamlet learns the distressing news from the Ghost that Claudius and Gertrude have plotted the murder of his father, the king; and the Ghost charges Hamlet with the duty to kill the usurping king, but Hamlet is to let heaven punish his mother.

Hamlet promises obedience to his murdered father's Ghost; however, his introspective nature causes him to want more proof. He pretends to be mad so that he might not arouse suspicion on the part of his mother and the King. Some of the members of the household assume that Hamlet's madness was a result of his "love-sick" emotional state. Since he previously had shown affection for Ophelia, the daughter of Polonius, who is the Lord Chamberlain, the young Hamlet would be expected to act a bit crazy if he were emotionally stricken by love. After Polonius instructs his daughter to be careful about further association with Hamlet, the young prince, with a sharp reprimand, tells Ophelia to get herself into a nunnery.

When Hamlet hears that a group of players are coming to perform at the castle, he questions them to ascertain if they are familiar with a certain play. "The Murder of Gonzago" would be the method by which Hamlet could catch the conscience of the king. In the meantime, Claudius has summoned two men who had been friends with Hamlet in his childhood days. Rosencrantz and Guildenstern are the perfect tools to take Hamlet away from the Danish castle, for Claudus is beginning to suspect that Hamlet may know far more than anyone may think. In other words, Hamlet is becoming a dangerous threat to his future.

The presentation of "The Murder of Gonzago" to the royal court has accomplished Hamlet's purpose. Following the play, Hamlet is now certain that Claudius and his mother are the murderers of his father. He must procrastinate no further. The play has also had a profound effect on the King. He rushes into the chapel, where he kneels in prayer trying to confess his sins. Hamlet passes by and sees his opportunity to take his revenge. Indecision again causes Hamlet to stop himself from carrying out his duty. He argues with himself that the deed should not be done while Claudius is in prayer, for it would be better to catch him in an evil act, and to kill him honorably. In fact, if he kills the king while he is praying, Hamlet might be sending the murderer's soul to heaven! It is in this discussion with his inner thoughts that the audience should view Hamlet as a tragic figure. He has rationalized away his best opportunity for carrying out his duty, which he had promised his father (the Ghost) he would do.

At this point, the play takes a very tragic turn. Hamlet, again disobeying his father, rushes to his mother's room to verbally chastise her. While there, he sees a movement behind the curtains, and, believing this to be the King, he stabs Polonius and kills him. King Claudius is now in control of events. Rosencrantz and Guildenstern bear letters to England that demand that Hamlet be put to death. The King sends Hamlet to England, but pirates capture his ship and return him unexpectedly to Denmark.

In the meantime, at Elsinore Castle, Ophelia is losing her mind and eventually dies by drowning. Her brother, Laertes, has heard the news that Hamlet has killed his father Polonius, so he is now bound by the revenge law to kill his father's murderer. Hamlet had finally realized that he had been thinking too precisely about his plans to kill Claudius. In his last soliloquy, Hamlet says: "How all occasions do inform against me and spur my dull revenge!"[16] He concludes the soliloquy with these words: "Oh, from this time forth, my thoughts be bloody or be nothing worth!"[17]

With full resolve to carry out his mission, Hamlet arrives at Elsinore. The King has already worked out a plan by which Laertes can kill Hamlet, and Laertes is prepared for the fight. Laertes is doubly possessed to exercise justice against Hamlet because of his sister's death, which he believed Hamlet caused. The King's plan is for Laertes and Hamlet to have a duel, during which Laertes will kill Hamlet with a poisoned rapier. Although Hamlet has resolved to complete his mission, he has a last minute of procrastination when he passes through the graveyard and picks up the skull of a jester he had especially loved when he was a boy. The "poor Yorick" speech provides the audience with comic relief before the final flow of blood during the duel.

In preparation for the fencing match, Laertes puts poison on the tip of his sword. But the King fears the plan may fail, so he poisons the cup from which Hamlet will drink to refresh himself. Laertes wounds Hamlet with his poisoned sword, but the swords are exchanged, and Hamlet strikes Laertes with a fatal blow. The Queen, by mistake, drinks from the goblet, and the dying Laertes exposes the evil deeds of Claudius. Hamlet has received his final confirmation. He takes the poisoned sword and stabs Claudius; then the prince forces the poisoned wine down the King's throat. He joins his queen in death. Laertes admits his sins and seeks forgiveness from the dying Hamlet. The King is dead, and Hamlet has fulfilled his mission, but the cost in lives far exceeded the plans his father (the Ghost) had laid out for him.

Hamlet has enough breath in him not only to forgive Laertes but also to assign to his close friend Horatio the commission to order the future of Denmark. He is to turn the throne over to young Fortinbras of Norway, whom Hamlet trusts to lead his country to a time of peace. An English ambassador enters the stage to announce that those two evil companions, Rosencrantz and Guildenstern, are dead. And so the tragedy ends with all the leading characters carried off the stage to be placed safely in their graves.

No play has ever been written which has provoked more discussion than *Hamlet*. However, we must be careful not to lose the original purpose of the play. Harrison has reminded us: "*Hamlet* is an Elizabethan play and not a Victorian treatise on philosophy or psychology, and that it was written to be acted in the Globe Theatre about 1600."[18]

With this in mind, I will not go on to a discussion of the theological and philosophical implications of the play. However, I do want to spell out some thoughts about Hamlet's character. He knew his station in life, which was a prince destined to become the next king. He had great respect for his father, but he was uncertain, at first, that the Ghost was actually that of his father. The murder of his father and the adultery of his mother were almost more than he could accept, for his sense of reality had been turned upside down.

In each of the eight soliloquies, the audience gains a deeper understanding of the pressures Hamlet faced. In the most famous one, he contemplates suicide. This, however, is not the reasoning of a man actually bent on killing himself. Rather, Hamlet is struggling with his reasons for going ahead with his mission. When he says, "Conscience doth make cowards of us all,"[19] there is no thought that he might actually label himself a coward. What he is saying is that tough responsibilities are not given to men of weak constitutions. Important matters must be carried out or we will lose our sense of action.

Again, the character flaw of indecision has become a roadblock to Hamlet's plan of action. In a previous soliloquy, the Prince of Denmark laments: "Oh, what a rogue and peasant slave am I!"[20] Here Hamlet admits that he has been a slave to his own character flaws, and now he must find a way to overcome his weaknesses. When tragedy strikes our lives, the easy thing to do is to give up. Hamlet may have put himself into some precarious predicaments, but he never really quits. He is a survivor until the final moment when he kills Claudius.

Howse believes the Hamlet story is a poor one: ". . . in spite of adultery, a mad woman, a fight in a grave, and eight violent deaths. But Shakespeare did not need much of a story. Here, as elsewhere, he uses the story simply as an operating table on which to dissect human character and to show what ruins and ennobles the lives of men and women."[21] There are many interpretations a director may give to this play. I have been rewarded by seeing various productions of *Hamlet*, which have opened a door for some interesting discussions about the deeper meanings in the soliloquies and some differences in opinion about character development in this drama.

When the student of Shakespeare has attained a certain amount of experience in reading, studying, discussing, viewing, or even acting in a play written by the world's greatest playwright, he develops an enjoyment and appreciation of great drama that is difficult to attain elsewhere. I shall never tire of *Hamlet*. Every time I work through this play, something I had not previously noticed before becomes evident. This is also true to a degree with all Shakespeare's plays, but *Hamlet* offers a special fascination unique to the stage. I have yet to see a presentation of *Hamlet* that meets my expectations in every degree. That is why I continue to teach the plays of Shakespeare in the classroom. There is always something to look forward to in every new class experience.

---

1 *Hamlet*, Act II, scene 2, lines 633–634.

2 Harrison, *Shakespeare, Major Plays,* 1948, 103.

3 Chute, *Stories from Shakespeare,* 1956, 274.

4 Harrison, 1948, 454.

5 Verna Hall, *The Christian History of the Constitution of the United States,* Vol. I: *Christian Self-Government.* San Francisco: Foundation for American Christian Education, 1966 & subsequent editions from Chesapeake, VA, 38.

6 *Henry V,* Act III, scene 1, line 1.

7 Ibid., Act II, scene 2. Cambridge, Scroop, and Grey have been arrested for high treason. King Henry hears the case and finds them guilty.

8 *Arthur's bosom*: Quickly actually means "Abraham's bosom," an idiom for "heaven."

9 *Henry V,* Act II, scene 3, lines 9–10.

10 Ibid., line 33.

11 *antics*: clowns.

12 *Henry V,* Act III, scene 2, lines 29–57.

13 *Henry V,* Act IV, scene 1, line 47.

14 Harrison, 1948, 602.

15 Howse, *Spiritual Values in Shakespeare,* 1955, 21.

16 *Hamlet*, Act IV, scene 4, lines 32–33.

17 Ibid., lines 65–66.

18 Harrison, 1948.

19 *Hamlet*, Act III, scene 1, line 83.

20 *Henry V,* Act II, scene 2, line 576.

21 Howse, 25.

Chapter Ten

"All the World's a Stage"

Shakespeare on the Stage

AQUES, a lord attending the banished duke in *As You Like It*, has one of the most beloved speeches in Shakespeare's works. It is called "The Seven Ages of Man," and takes a male figure from birth to death, with comical remarks at each stage of his life. When our class determined to put this play on the stage, I immediately began casting the role in my mind. Who could best deliver this important speech? It had to be a boy with excellent abilities of sensitivity and a slight adaptation toward joking. On the third row, front seat, sat Randy Green, star soccer player and very popular with both guys and gals in the school.

After school one day, I called to him, put the script in front of him, and said, "Randy, read this speech for me." He was made for the speech and the speech was made for him. I knew I had a winner. Randy was a very fine Jaques. He was also introspective enough to dig into the depths of a very complicated character. Now I needed to find his partner in comedy. Craig Newman had been in my classes for a couple of years, and he had always shown an affinity for acting. As we worked through the play in class, I noticed that he was very fond of the Touchstone role.

Now Touchstone needs some very special abilities. There have been times when I have been concerned about the interpretation of Touchstone I had seen in other productions, but there was one that caught my imagination. Touchstone is thoroughly English in a very proper way so that he shows a somewhat stuffy and egotistic manner, looking down on persons without proper breeding. Craig could do it. He even invented a special accent for the part. But I had to help him use the accent with proper and overdone enunciation so that the audience would not miss a single word.

The two anchors were set. The inner play and humor between these two characters can carry the play, as long as the other actors respond properly to their antics. Rosalind and Celia, the two leading ladies, must have a natural attraction to each other, much as two very close sisters would have. Again we had two naturals. Rosalind has an enormous amount of lines in this play, so I needed to find a girl who could memorize quickly. Stephanie Siemens was the girl who was the most efficient at memorization of any student I had ever had in a Shakespeare class. And she was almost in love with the part. Furthermore, she knew just who could play Celia.

Hope Wieneke already had a special affection for Stephanie, and the two were naturals working together. There was one problem. The school had academic standards for students involved in extra-curricular activities. Hope was slightly below the minimum grade point level required to be in the play. This meant many extra hours on my part, helping her to raise her grades to the place where the school would give its approval. But it was worth it. I knew these two girls working together would bring a certain flavor to our production that would not have been possible with any other combination of girls in the school.

This play requires twenty-nine actors, if every person takes only one role. I decided that some actors would need to play two roles because American Heritage was a small high school. Another problem for our school also became evident: the enrollment showed a smaller number of boys than girls. As is commonly known, Shakespeare wrote his plays for a male cast only. Young boys took the women's roles, and these were limited. Some changes in the casting had to be made. We changed several male parts to female by making very slight changes in the names. For example, Amiens became Amiena. Rebekah Alexander was a young lady who was quite tall and had a deep voice. With a beard and voice work to make her sound like a man, she took the part of Corin, an older shepherd.

Orlando and Duke Senior are very important character roles. They must be cast correctly. Mike Gonzáles would make a great Orlando, but he had already designed the portable stage and was set to be the Stage Manager. Still he wanted to play opposite Stephanie, and I was convinced he was perfect for the part. Mike was able to convince his good friend, Marc Davilla, to take over the work of Stage Manager so that he could assume the role of Orlando. I will always be indebted to those two really great guys for their loyalty and commitment, which was invaluable to the success of the play.

One day I was watching a soccer game at the school, and I noticed a blond-haired boy sitting on the sidelines. Since I had never met him, I walked up to him, and asked: "Don't you like to play soccer?" He quickly informed me that he had transferred into our school too late to try out for the team. I introduced myself as the faculty member who taught Shakespeare, and he responded with so much enthusiasm, I said to myself, "This guy has some acting talent." Dale Bonds would not only prove to be extremely talented, but he also had the ability to undertake a variety of roles. The next fall, he signed up for my Shakespeare class. I knew immediately he could handle the Duke Senior role.

Dale was one of the hardest workers I had ever coached in drama. Furthermore, he was a perfectionist. Working with Dale Bonds was one of my most enjoyable tasks in all my years of teaching. He was also an outstanding student. However, I was soon to learn that he was not so committed in some of his other classes. Other faculty members warned me that he might not be able to keep up his grade point average, and the faculty recommended that Dale should not take on this demanding role since he might have to drop out of the play. At this point it could be too late to substitute another student. My next step was to have a heart-to-heart talk with Dale about doing well in all his subjects. Dale accepted the challenge, and I will never regret standing by him.

The role of Duke Senior is so important, because the actor must understand how his brother, Duke Frederick, had unjustly seized his lands and dukedom and banished him forever from his kingdom. Moreover, the cast member who plays this part has the task of convincing an audience how God had taught him to be happy in his primitive circumstances. Dale had his audiences spellbound when he spoke the following lines:

> Sweet are the uses of adversity,
> Which, like the toad, ugly and venomous,
> Wears yet a precious jewel in his head.
> And this our life exempt from public haunt
> Finds tongues in trees, books in running brooks,
> Sermons in stones, and good in everything.
> I would not change it.[1]

At the first evening performance, when Dale concluded his speech, there was a hush over the auditorium. I was thinking: "Amiena, don't respond too soon." All of a sudden, the entire audience reacted with resounding applause. Amiena didn't seem to know what to do next. Sometimes, players will move into their next lines before the audience stops clapping, and the words are lost. This is one of those moments when directors worry about the lack of stage experience on the part of high school students. However, Chrissie Ellis collected herself, walked to the front of the stage, pulling Dale along with her, and motioned to the audience to quiet down. I began to realize that I had another future actress in this bright young lady, who responded with equal clarity:

> Happy is your Grace,
> That can translate the stubbornness of fortune
> Into so quiet and so sweet a style.[2]

Since Chrissie was only a sophomore, I was already making plans in my mind for her senior year performance. The reason Chrissie had been selected for this part was that the actor is required to sing, and she had a lovely soprano voice with some experience in singing solos in the school choir. My next step in making decisions for this production was the music. Amiena, Hymena, and the pages have choral numbers. So I made a phone call to Ashland to ask about music for *As You Like It*. I did not get the answer I had hoped for. What I had requested was the music from their last performance of *As You Like It*. The answer I got: "Dr.

Bowmer's policy has always been to have new music composed each time the company produced a new version of a Shakepeare play, and we recommend that you do the same."

American Heritage had been blessed with an extremely talented faculty that year. Our music teacher, Mr. David Krebs, was a gifted composer. After I had explained the situation, he graciously agreed to compose music in the Elizabethan mode. The result was fabulous. Since I already had a soprano soloist, my next task was to identify pages who could sing. This meant that we would need younger boys, students from the junior high, but the principal was not too pleased to have any involvement with a senior high play. My son, Mark, had a fine high soprano voice, and his younger brother, Tom, had sung a duet with him in the past. The principal agreed that as long as I did not involve any other junior high students, she would allow me to use my own sons as pages.

If my students had not been so insistent, I would never have started my directing career with a play as complex as this. This, however, was not my first attempt at directing. I had, in fact, directed many church plays and YMCA productions over the years, but it was my first opportunity to tackle a Shakespearean production. I would much rather have begun with a play like *Love's Labor's Lost* or *A Midsummer Night's Dream*. Nevertheless, this class was an exceptional group, and I wanted to serve them.

One more extremely vital part of the play had not yet been assigned. The role of Oliver de Boys needed an actor with the ability to convince an audience that he had been converted from an evil, despotic figure into a loyal and loving brother who is fully repentant of his sinful deeds. A certain amount of make-up would help, but the actor must be convincing. Richard Fong agreed to try his skill at this demanding role. For some time, during rehearsals I felt he was not thoroughly convincing. Not until dress rehearsal did I give a sigh of relief. Some actors, especially amateurs and children, never seem to be able to do their best until they get into full production. Suddenly, in full costume, with all the stage lights on, they rise to the occasion. Here is a wonderful play about conversion, and the audience deserves to see the formerly wicked man changed into the new-born man in Christ.

Another important role, although it has only a few lines, is that of Jaques de Boys. He is the man who gives the news that the renegade Duke Frederick has been converted. How many times I have seen this play, and the most important lines are missed by the audience. I was determined that this would not be the case in our production. So I called on my own son, David, who has attended Shakespeare plays from the time he was five. He would take the role of Dennis, a servant to Oliver, in the first part of the play, and then return as Jaques de Boys in the last scene. What a privilege to have all three of my sons taking part in my first Shakespeare play!

The role of Duke Frederick required an actor who could make the audience dislike him from the moment he enters the stage. Roy Littwin was a military-minded young man, whose outward appearance gave the impression he was much older than his actual age. He was perfect in a role where he could rant and rage to his heart's content. Fortunately, Roy would not have to appear on stage as the converted Duke.

Another small role that required a very special type of acting is that of Monsieur Le Beau, a fantastical Frenchman. This is not the kind of part most high school boys want to play, but, when done with finesse, Le Beau is a big hit. My son, David, had a close friend, John Overy, who was also in his class at American Heritage. John seemed to have the right stuff, and I didn't think he would mind the effeminate nature of Le Beau's character. Our costume manager found just the right costume: a blue top, with black tights and a marvelous French (white) wig. Then he would carry around the proverbial white handkerchief, waving it about at the proper moments. John Overy showed in his mastery of this role that he was destined for greater parts in the future.

The humor in this play requires good acting in all the little roles where the actor is onstage briefly. We still had to fill the roles of Charles, the wrestler; Adam, the faithful servant to Orlando; Silvius, a love-sick shepherd; Audrey, a country wench; Sir Oliver Martext, a mixed-up vicar; William, a plain country fellow who likes Audrey; Hymena, the

Shakespeare for Everyone to Enjoy

goddess of marriage; and Phoebe, the shepherdess who falls in love with Ganymede (Rosalind in disguise) and who is the object of Silvius' affection. Again, just the right young people became available to help give the play its finishing touches.

John Wiggs, who had failed my Latin class in a previous term, was another student who had to improve his grades. I give a lot of credit to John for his cooperation, and I believe this experience helped turn his life around. He was a most wonderful Silvius, pursuing the lovely girl of his dreams, Phoebe, acted by Lori Gaustad, and I can still hear his great lines ringing in my ears: "Oh Phoebe, Phoebe, Phoebe!"[3]

Steve Dunn, a young man whose devotion to the Lord was a sterling example before the entire student body, took the part of Adam. Steve effectively performed this role of the tired old servant of Sir Rowland de Boys, who was faithful to Orlando when the whole world seemed to turn against his beloved master. Two years later, Steve would take the role of the Jew, Tubal, playing opposite his brother Mark as Shylock in *The Merchant of Venice*.

Keith Perkins, in the role of Sir Oliver Martext, gave a fine rendition of his interchange with Touchstone on the meaning of marriage, in a most humorous fashion. William, acted by Phil White, could not win Audrey, played by Monica Hurt, away from Touchstone, although he had considered Touchstone an intruder to the Forest. Touchstone, having won Audrey's heart, was happy to learn that Sir Oliver was somewhat inept. After all, he reasoned, if the vicar should exhibit a weak performance in his marriage ceremony, this would mean that the knot would not be tied so tight that Touchstone could not break it, if for some reason after they had left the Forest for the formal Court, Audrey might turn out to be too far below Touchstone's social standing. An interesting note regarding Touchstone and Audrey: several years later Craig Newman (Touchstone) and Monica (Audrey) married, and today they are raising a fine Christian family.

The professional wrestler, Charles, required an actor with a strong body, who would appear to be the overwhelming favorite in a match with

Orlando. Ray Vermillion looked the part, but could he make the audience believe that Orlando would very likely lose, or might even be killed? After a period of working with Ray, we concluded both Ray and Mike needed wrestling lessons if this match were to be done effectively. The pastor of the Baptist Church in Newark, Jerry Martin, had many years experience teaching wrestling, and he agreed to be our wrestling coach. In order to emphasize the excitement of the match, I instructed the actors to run down the center aisle of the auditorium, shouting out commands to other cast members to join in the fun by rooting for their favorite wrestler. Orlando, of course, wins the match, but his brother Oliver banishes him from the Court.

This banishment is necessary to put Orlando and Adam into the Forest of Arden. Duke Frederick, when he had stolen the kingdom away from his brother, banished Duke Senior from the palace and all the kingdom's lands. When the play opens, Duke Senior and his loyal lords have been living in the Forest of Arden for many years. After the duke had sent Orlando away from his home, he decides to give Rosalind, Duke Senior's daughter, a notice of banishment. Celia, Duke Frederick's daughter, and Rosalind's cousin and lifelong friend, cannot bear to be separated. Therefore, they ask the Court Jester, Touchstone, to accompany them. Rosalind decides to take on the disguise of the boy Ganymede, and Celia takes the female disguise of Aliena. Together the three start out for the Forest of Arden.

This place is no ordinary forest. It is a place of suffering and trials that work on changing the character of those who go there. The Forest of Arden speaks messages of truth to those who have the ears to listen. So in this magical land of truth, far different from the false Court, reality works its way into the hearts of those who come there, although some who come this way might not see the beauty at first. Touchstone's first remarks about the forest show his initial dislike for the place:

> Aye, now am I in Arden, the more fool I.
> When I was at home, I was in a better place.
> But travelers must be content.[4]

Shakespeare for Everyone to Enjoy

Once Touchstone has begun to adjust to his new life in the forest, he meets Jaques, the lord whose melancholy humor has been entertaining the banished duke. Jaques is so taken with Touchstone that he reports back to Duke Senior with his amazing discovery:

> A fool, a fool! I met a fool i' the forest,
> A motley fool, a miserable world!
> As I do live by food, I met a fool,
> Who laid him down and basked him in the sun,
> And railed on Lady Fortune in good terms,
> In good set terms, and yet a motley fool. . . .[5]

What the audience learns from these inspiring lines is that wisdom often comes from fools, at least from the fools in Shakespeare's plays. Both Touchstone and Jaques are fools of a different type. Jaques is the intellectual, melancholy fool, whose wisdom results from his hours of railing at nature. It is Jaques that delivers that most famous of all speeches, "All the world's a stage, and all the men and women merely players. . . ."[6] This presentation of the seven stages of a man's life depicts with humor and wisdom the philosophy that life could be without any great meaning, except that the events of a man's life in the Forest of Arden can bring such character development that life may be seen from another perspective. What happens to a man's future when he is converted from his former selfish existence to a man who sees beauty and goodness in even the harshness of nature?

The power of the Forest brings together in life commitment four couples: Orlando and Rosalind, Oliver and Celia, Silvius and Phebe, Touchstone and Audrey. Duke Senior would never have desired to return to the formal Court. Oliver has repented his former life of selfishness and greed, and Duke Frederick would restore the lands he has stolen to his brother. But that is not quite enough. The melancholy Jaques is fully convinced that there is much to learn from those whose lives have been so dramatically changed.

The blessings of Hymena, goddess of marriage (played by Jamie Martin), are spoken over the newly-married couples, which concludes with a wedding song. Again, the casting required a contralto soloist to contrast with Chrissie's high soprano. Because our school was blessed with an especially good music program, we had an opportunity to embellish our production with extra fine music. The play concludes with a dance performed by the newlyweds. Bob Vinson, a member of my congregation in Union City, volunteered to serve as the dance instructor. These four newlywed couples were the center of a wedding dance, which concluded the play, except for Rosalind's final speech, which is the Epilogue.

We had worked on a variety of curtain calls, in the event that the audience would call the cast back to the stage. At the last evening performance, there was a lengthy standing ovation, during which all the curtain calls were needed. Our first Shakespeare production had been an outstanding success, far beyond my expectations. As I mentioned in a previous chapter, I would not take on the job of directing unless the school could find a producer, whose work is infinitely more time consuming than that of the director. Kathryn Johnson, parent of one of our students, had many years of experience, and was pleased to be asked to be our producer.

The tasks of the producer involve literally every aspect of the play that is not directly related to the acting. Mrs. Johnson, however, also volunteered her time to be a drama coach. With so many different roles (twenty-nine in all), a production of this immensity requires several coaches to see that every character is achieving the effect required for my standard of perfection. We worked the entire year, and scheduled our performances for the next-to-last week of the school year.

It is the producer who oversees the hours and hours of planning and just plain hard work. The cooperation on the part of students, faculty, parents, and friends was well worth it. A stage had been built. Some of the Elizabethan costumes were rented, but students and staff helped to make some of them by hand. All the scenery was designed and created by the art department. Mrs. Johnson also worked with our talented music department that was in charge of writing and directing the live music. She also helped Mr. Krebs, who coordinated the Elizabethan recorded music, which was played as the audiences were gathering, and at certain spots in the play, where the actors needed time to move on stage. In addition to all this, the producer must arrange for publicity, ticket sales, and refreshments during our two intermissions. (Because the play runs almost three hours in length, it was necessary to schedule two intermissions of ten minutes each.) Then she must oversee the ushers, the sound and lighting technicians, the prompters, and staff to be in charge of the dressing rooms.

A small Christian high school had proven that Shakespeare could be staged and presented to an audience, most of whom had never seen a live Shakespeare performance. Although some of those who attended thought the play ran just a bit too long, most of the response was gratifying. The school leadership was so impressed with the outcome of our first attempt at putting a Shakespeare play on our school stage that another play was scheduled for the following year; however, I was physically and emotionally exhausted from this production. For our next presentation, I chose one of Shakespeare's shortest plays, *The Comedy of Errors*.

The joy of putting Shakespeare on the stage remains strong in my memory, so much so that I would like to challenge others to stage a Shakespeare play. Whether you are part of a homeschool group or attend high school or college, the experience of acting in one of these wonderful plays is most rewarding. Church groups or little theater groups often do the Bard's plays quite well. My experience is, that with the exception of the Oregon Shakespeare Festival in Ashland, and of course, the Royal Shakespeare Company in Britain, some of the most enjoyable experiences are provided by amateur groups. As we leave the stage, I quote the words of Jaques:

> All the world's a stage,
> And all the men and women merely players.
> They have their exits and their entrances,
> And one man in his time plays many parts,
> His acts being seven ages. As, first the infant,
> Mewling and puking in his nurse's arms,
> Then the whining schoolboy, with his satchel

And shining morning face, creeping like snail
Unwilling to school. And then the lover,
Sighing like furnace, with a woeful ballad
Made to his mistress' eyebrow. Then a soldier,
Full of strange oaths and bearded like the pard,
Jealous in honor, sudden and quick in quarrel,
Seeking the bubble reputation
Even in the cannon's mouth. And then the justice,
In fair round belly with good capon lined,
With eyes severe and beard of formal cut,
Full of wise saws and modern instances,
And so he plays his part. The sixth age shifts
Into the lean and slippered Pantaloon
With spectacles on nose and pouch on side,
His youthful hose, well saved, a world too wide
For his shrunk shank, and his big manly voice,
Turning again toward childish treble, pipes
And whistles in his sound. Last scene of all,
That ends this strange eventful history,
Is second childishness and mere oblivion,
Sans teeth, sans eyes, sans taste, sans everything.[7]

Putting Shakespeare on the stage had been an underlying desire for
Angus Bowmer when he became a teacher in the English Department
at Southern Oregon Normal School in Ashland. In fact, Bowmer tells
us, in his autobiography, *As I Remember, Adam,* that this school had neither a drama department nor a speech department, with little prospect
for the development of either. When Dr. Bowmer was hired to teach
in Ashland, the school was only six years old. It was a two-year school
of almost three hundred students, designed for the purpose of training
grade-school teachers. Dr. Bowmer said he was horrified when he first
saw the school auditorium.[8]

But Angus Bowmer was an overcomer. Difficulties with terrible
auditoriums only seemed to strengthen his resolve. Since he was not able
to start the Festival until four years later, although he did not realize the
importance of that time period, it was invaluable for laying the ground-

Shakespeare for Everyone to Enjoy

work for what was to become the Oregon Shakespeare Festival. As we have pointed out in an earlier chapter, Iden Payne had first inspired Angus Bowmer to want to work on an Elizabethan-type stage with period costumes. In fact, it was from Dr. Payne that he had learned that "Shakespeare was something to be done, not written about."[9]

This lovely little town of Ashland, Oregon, actually has had a history of entertainment and drama. In the late 1800s, the Chautauqua building was erected in Ashland to draw crowds from Oregon and Northern California to see performances of plays, as well as opera singers, and orators such as William Jennings Bryan and Billy Sunday. But the Chautauqua organization died out. The huge dome of the building was removed, and only the exterior walls were left standing. In the ruins of this old building, Dr. Bowmer could imagine a Shakespearean stage, which could be used to produce plays.

The old exterior Chautauqua walls still stand, and form the exterior of the outdoor Elizabethan theater. Angus Bowmer's dream had come to fruition. From its small beginnings in 1935, the Festival now has one of the largest audiences in America. Not only are Shakespeare's plays produced on the Elizabethan stage, but they are also performed in the Bowmer and New Theatres.

John Gielgud in his book, *Acting Shakespeare*, spells out the importance of putting Shakespeare on the stage. Although he is willing to write about it, where Iden Payne wanted to concentrate on doing Shakespeare, the stage is his great love. Dr. Baxter used to say that John Gielgud was the best Hamlet he had ever seen. Gielgud says: "My parents took me to see Shakespeare sometimes when I was a boy, but I was chiefly attracted . . . by the scenery and costumes and romantic atmosphere . . . I find that I have to be involved in a play in order to become absorbed by it, and I feel somewhat ashamed never to have appreciated the work of Beckett and Brecht, since I think if I had ever acted in one of their plays I might have learned to understand them better, as I did with Shakespeare."[10]

The important lesson from Sir John Gielgud is that when an actor is involved with Shakespeare on the stage, the joy turns to love. The experience of directing a play was even more powerful than just acting in it. Sir John reports that he has directed eight of Shakespeare's plays, and that he has come to appreciate the depth and enjoyment of these projects because he would be actually experiencing the power of the message. Also he has come to find great pleasure even in the rehearsals. Here the director has the opportunity to set the tone and create a good atmosphere for both actors and designers.[11]

Although I have never met John Gielgud, I have had the opportunity to see his work in a few non-Shakespeare productions. I have also seen him on film as Cassius in *Julius Caesar*. I often have wished I could have seen him on stage in at least one of his Shakespeare plays, for I am convinced that he is one of the greatest Shakespearean actors of our time. His work has inspired many other actors and directors who are interested in putting the Bard's plays on the stage, so that there is a continuing interest in introducing Shakespeare to those who have never seen his plays.

---

1 *As You Like It,* Act II, scene 1, lines 12–18.

2 Ibid., scene 1, lines 19–20.

3 Ibid., scene 4, line 43.

4 Ibid., scene 4, lines 16–18.

5 Ibid., scene 7, lines 12–16.

6 Ibid., scene 7, lines 139-140.

7 Ibid., scene 7, lines 139–160.

8 Bowmer, *As I Remember, Adam,* Ashland, Oregon: The Oregon Shakespeare Festival Association, 39. Note: The title of Dr. Bowmer's book is actually the first line of the play, *As You Like It.*

9 Ibid., 25.

10 John Gielgud, *Acting Shakespeare,* N.Y.: Charles Scribner's Sons, 1991, ix–x.

11 Ibid., 34–37.

Chapter Eleven

"All's Well that Ends Well"

Conclusion

*A*s we pointed out in the introductory chapter of this book, Shakespeare had one major motive in writing his plays: to entertain. Furthermore, he sought to use his plays to bring enjoyment to all classes of people, from the groundlings to royalty. Very few playwrights have been as successful in reaching such a wide variety of persons. Not only was he the most popular writer of his day, but also his plays have continued to delight audiences since that time. Even more people today would find genuine entertainment in his plays if they were able to discover a new interest in some of the finest literature ever written.

To develop an interest in Shakespeare's works, it is important to seek opportunities for a serious study of his plays. If a class on Shakespeare is not available or convenient for a busy schedule, I suggest that the reader search out some excellent material that helps explain the play. Although many teachers do not like their students to use *Cliffs Notes,*[1] I have always encouraged my students to read them, compare the material with what they learned in class, and then come to their own personal conclusions.

If the student is not able to study under a teacher who has had formal training in explaining details and elaborating on the meaning of the plays, he should seek out other students who might wish to discuss the plays in a group study. In fact, a study group could read the plays aloud, each member taking the various parts, working through one play. I suggest that you start with one of the less complicated plays, such as *The Comedy of Errors, The Taming of the Shrew,* or *A Midsummer Night's Dream.* Next, you might want to try reading through one of the histories. *Richard*

II and *Richard III* are good starting points. Then, I suggest you pick one of the simpler tragedies: *Romeo and Juliet* or *Macbeth*.

After the group has studied and discussed a play, the next step should be to go to the play on stage, if it is scheduled in your community. If not, there are several plays available on video. Sometimes, in my classes, we would study a play, see the video, and then go to the theater to see the live performance. The value of a live presentation of the play is that the actors interact with the audience.

Do not allow a poor performance of any play to cause you to form a dislike for Shakespeare. In every production there is often some redeeming value. The actors may not have interpreted the play to your satisfaction. Or perhaps the director did not seem to understand the main focus of the play. Sometimes the cast simply has a bad night. Whatever may happen when you attend the play, you have an opportunity to gain something. Especially if you go with a group, and then schedule a discussion following the performance, you will create an opportunity to evaluate what you have seen and how this affects your understanding of the play as a whole.

Even in some of the worst presentations, where the setting seemed to be out of context with the intent of the playwright, or several of the actors did not appear to grasp the depth of their character, I have observed some of the best characterizations of a particular role that I have ever seen. A few years ago, I attended a production of *Romeo and Juliet* where the setting and the costumes were worse than usual. But the role of the Nurse was superb. The actress was somewhat heavyset and dominated the stage. She wore a dress that was intended to cover up her weight and waddled across the stage in high heels. A tragedy needs some moments of tragic relief. This Nurse was so hysterically funny, that just her appearance on the stage brought forth thunderous laughter from the audience. What made this role so delightful to me is that I had never before seen this characterization of the Nurse, although I have attended countless performances of *Romeo and Juliet*.

At another time we saw a production in Ashland of *As You Like It*, which was fairly well done but lacked the polish of a top presentation. First of all, I did not care for the setting, which was in the outdoor Elizabethan theater. Another stage had been erected over the original stage so that it was more like an indoor theater. I especially enjoy the Elizabethan stage, with its various levels and entrances so that the play can make use of the entire stage. This setting, to me, limited the action so that it could have just as easily been performed in the indoor theater.

Secondly, for a play like *As You Like It*, I prefer to see it in Elizabethan costume or at least some historical period costumes. Although the costumes were colorful, I had difficulty determining what period the director had intended for the setting. It may have been in a more modern setting, although the costumes did not especially lend themselves to a contemporary setting. It is possible that the setting had been used in an indoor theater and then transferred to the outdoor stage. Although the use of costumes was not inappropriate, I found myself having trouble adjusting to the play as it began.

Thirdly, many of the main characters seemed distracted and unable to lure me into a character study. One of the things I enjoy the most in seeing the Bard's plays is being able to identify at least with the main characters. Live theater can change from night to night because there are many circumstances that determine the outcome. Sometimes, the actors must put up with a "dead" audience. Nothing the actors do seems to arouse them, and the interaction with the audience falls flat.

However, in this particular performance, two actors stood out. The interpretation of Touchstone (the clown or fool) was done with intricate detail in a manner that I had always admired. Touchstone has so many great lines, and he can be one of the most humorous characters in all Shakespeare. This Touchstone was sharp and intensely funny. He knew exactly when to pause and when to move rapidly. He was worth the price of admission. The following dialogue will illustrate Touchstone's wit.

> JAQUES: But for the seventh cause, how did you find the quarrel on the seventh cause?
>
> TOUCHSTONE: Upon the lie seven times removed—Bear your body more seeming, Audrey—as thus, sir, I did dislike the cut of a

certain courtier's beard. He sent me word if I said that his beard was not cut well, he was in the mind it was. This is called the Retort Courteous. If I sent him word again "it was not well cut," he would send me word to cut it to please himself. This is called the Quip Modest. If again "it was not well cut," he disabled my judgment. This is called the Reply Churlish. If again "it was not well cut," he would answer I spake not true. This is called the Reproof Valiant. If again "it was not well cut," he would say I lie. This is called the Countercheck Quarrelsome. And so to the lie Circumstantial and the Lie Direct.

JAQUES: And how oft did you say his beard was not well cut?

TOUCHSTONE: I durst go no further than the Lie Circumstantial, nor he durst not give me the Lie Direct, and so we measured swords and parted.[2]

Touchstone goes on to list in order the degrees of the lie in a most comical fashion so that Jaques replies to Duke Senior, "Is not this a rare fellow, my lord? He's as good at anything, and yet a fool."[3]

The second character that really caught my attention in this production was the role of Celia. Whereas the actor who portrayed Touchstone presented an interpretation exactly as I would have expected, the actress who played Celia gave an entirely new (to me) rendition that opened up some interesting aspects of her character that I had never imagined. The actress portrayed Celia as much less formal, with a flamboyant flair that totally dominated the stage in such a way that she added greatly to the comedy. The only problem was that she upstaged Rosalind, who is the female lead character in this play. However, I suspected that this was to some degree Rosalind's fault. For the actress who played the part of Rosalind never seemed to take charge, which is essential for the movement of the action.

What I have attempted to show is that even when you attend a Shakespearean play and it does not measure up to your highest expectations, look for other details that might help you appreciate the play itself. Every time you see the same play in a different setting, you should learn more about the principles and characters as well as the plot. This was part of the genius of Shakespeare. I have seen many productions of most of the great playwright's works and every one of the canon of thirty-seven plays at least twice. I never tire of seeing the most popular plays many times, because each time I see one, it becomes a new adventure for me.

The one aspect of some productions of which you must beware is a reading into the script of false concepts. These are ideas that Shakespeare never intended to be put into his plays, but they are not always easy to detect; and often you may not detect them unless you have gained a good understanding of the play as Shakespeare wrote it.

Recently I heard about a video production of *The Merchant of Venice*, which contains a false interpretation of the character of Antonio. Although I have never seen this video, I have been told that he is portrayed as having a homosexual infatuation with Bassanio. The rationale is that Antonio, the merchant of Venice, would never have taken such a risk to borrow the money from Shylock unless he and Bassanio were sexually involved. The truth of the matter is that Antonio loved Bassanio dearly, and was willing to risk his life for his friend.[4] Furthermore, since Bassanio wants to borrow the money so that he can go to Belmont to woo Portia, it is hardly rational to think that Bassanio would be physically attracted to Antonio or vice versa.

When I was in college, I took a New Testament class, in which the professor explained that there are two ways to interpret Scripture: by *exegesis*, reading out of the Scripture the true intent; the other method he called *eisegesis*, that is, reading into a passage something that is not there. My professor warned us that "reading in" was dangerous and to be avoided. I believe that some students of Shakespeare have a tendency to read into the text ideas that never crossed the Bard's mind.

Often the things that are read into the plays are characterizations or ideas that the reader actually imagines to be a part of the play as originally written; however, a careful study of the details would show that neither the plot nor the context would support these inventions. This is obvious when I see a production of a play in which one or more of the characters simply do not fit the text or the theme of the play. How could a good student of Shakespeare find a homosexual relationship between Antonio and Bassanio to have any real purpose in the plot or theme of *The Merchant of Venice*?

When Shakespeare wants to portray a character with homosexual or effeminate tendencies, he writes this into the character's description, although he may do this in a very subtle way. I cannot find any of these subtleties in the character of Antonio, and such tactics always weaken the main force of the play. Any production of a Shakespeare play must display a smooth transition from scene to scene so that the audience is not distracted by trivia or some other factor never intended by the writer. When the play flows, and each character brings the audience into the play so that everything from the minutest detail adds to the experience, then the audience is pleased.

A few years ago I had the fortune of attending a production of *A Midsummer Night's Dream* on the outdoor Elizabethan stage at Ashland that was extraordinary. Every costume, each tiny piece of scenery, the lighting and sound effects, all blended together into a tapestry of enjoyment. Every actor spoke with excellent diction so that we understood every word. This took place on a beautiful warm summer evening. Even using an older gentleman, Sandy McCallum, to take the role of Puck seemed to make that particular production almost magical. One of my sons said to me following the performance, "Dad, I never really liked this play when I saw it before. At those productions, I don't think I really grasped what Shakespeare intended when he wrote *A Midsummer Night's Dream*, but this production was great!"

There is such great satisfaction when we experience a Shakespeare play done to perfection. It does not happen as often as I would like. However, the Oregon Shakespeare Festival is the one acting company in America that in my experience more often reaches these heights in Elizabethan drama. Every year at Ashland there is usually one play, and sometimes several, that produces the desired satisfaction of seeing the works of Shakespeare as he intended them to be performed.

Whatever happens in your pursuit to understand and enjoy the works of Shakespeare, make a plan and stick to it. It is easy to get discouraged, especially if you do not have support from your associates. Remember that the Bard's plays have delighted generations of students and theater-goers. Why should you not benefit from the works of the greatest playwright who has ever lived? The end result is worth the struggle, and it may not even be a struggle. You may have missed the fun and excitement because you had no one to challenge you to get involved. If nothing else, I hope I have opened up an interest for you to explore a part of life you may have missed, or thought not worth your while.

One of the last plays that Shakespeare wrote is entitled *All's Well that Ends Well*. The play has a plot that seems to be leading the characters toward an increasingly hopeless conclusion. However, Shakespeare, through his ingenious ability to take what appears to be a situation so filled with confusion and sadness, unravels the plot so that everything works to a satisfactory conclusion. In spite of all the terrible events that have occurred in the past, nothing but happiness remains in the end. In the Epilogue, the King says:

> The king's a beggar, now the play is done.
> All is well ended, if this suit be won,
> That you express content; which we will pay,
> With strife to please you, day exceeding day.
> Ours be your patience then, and yours our parts;
> Your gentle hands lend us, and take our hearts.[5]

---

1 *Cliffs Notes* are published by Cliffs Notes, Lincoln, Nebraska, and edited by Gary Carey and James L. Roberts. Each play's notes are published separately under the name of that specific play.

2 *As You Like It,* Act V, scene 4, lines 69–92.

3 Ibid., scene 4, lines 109, 110.

4 Because Antonio's fortune was invested in ships, all of which were at sea, he found it necessary to borrow money from Shylock, the Jew. Shylock demanded as surety for the loan a pound of Antonio's flesh, taken anywhere from Antonio's body that Shylock demands.

5 *All's Well that Ends Well,* Act V, scene 3, lines 335–340.

Shakespeare's Birthplace

The Room in which Shakespeare was born

Appendix I

Records of the Life of Shakespeare

Excerpt from the General Introduction (Section 2 "Records of the Life of Shakespeare") in *Shakespeare: Major Plays and the Sonnets* by G. B. Harrison, copyright 1948 by Harcourt, Inc. and renewed 1975 by G. B. Harrison, reprinted by permission of the publisher.

*A*PART from the legends, inferences, interpretations, and deductions of scholars and critics, the actual facts of Shakespeare's life, duly authenticated in indisputable records, are considerable. A student of Shakespeare should know where fact ends and guessing begins. In this chapter, facts only are given. The more important records, most of which mention Shakespeare by name, are as follows:*

1564. APRIL 26. The parish register of the Stratford-on-Avon church records the baptism of "Guliemus filius Johannes Shakspere"—William son of John Shakspere.

There is no record of the date of birth, though Shakespeare's birthday is celebrated at Stratford-on-Avon and elsewhere on April 23, principally because this happens also to be the day of Saint George, the patron saint of England.

John Shakespeare had come to Stratford in the 1550s. He is variously described in records as yeoman (that is, a landowner), glover, and whitawer (one who cured glove skins). He had married Mary Arden, whose family were Roman Catholic gentlefolk living at Wilmcote near Stratford. John Shakespeare became a leading citizen of Stratford. In 1564 he was chosen alderman, and in 1568 bailiff—the highest civic office in the town, the modern mayor. After 1577 the records show that he was disposing of his property and had ceased to attend meetings of the corporation. In 1587 another was chosen alderman in his place. In 1592 his name appeared in the list of those in Stratford who absented themselves from church, and it was noted that he and others "came not to church for fear of process for debt."

1582. NOVEMBER 28. A license was issued by the bishop of Worcester to "William Shagspere" and "Anne Hathwey of Stratford" to solemnize matrimony upon once asking of the banns, provided that there was no legal objection.

The law required that the banns of marriage should be read out in church for three successive Sundays before the marriage. This was to enable anyone to show cause (such as precontract) why the marriage could not lawfully take place. When

---

* The spellings in records noted within quotes are original. There is no significance in the different spellings of Shakespeare's name; his contemporaries were very free in such matters. Indeed, I have encountered a case where a Lord Lieutenant of a county signed his own name in three different spellings on the same day in one set of documents. Marlowe's name appears in different documents as Marlo, Marle, Marley, Marlin, Merling, Marling, Morley. In Shakespeare's will, the scribe spelt the name of "Shackspeare" on the first sheet and "Shackspere" on the third. Shakespeare himself signed the three sheets: on the first he wrote "William Shakspere," on the second "Willm̄ Shakspere," on the third "By me William Shakspere."

for any reason the parties wished to hasten the marriage, a special license from the bishop was required.

According to the inscription on the grave of Anne Shakespeare, she died on August 6, 1623, aged sixty-seven years. She was therefore born in 1556, and was thus eight years older than her husband.

1583. MAY 26. The parish register of the Stratford-on-Avon church records the baptism of Susanna, daughter to William Shakespeare.

1585. FEBRUARY 2. The parish register of the Stratford-on-Avon church records the baptism of "Hamnet & Judeth, sonne and daughter to William Shakspere."

1588. MICHAELMAS. John and Mary Shakespeare claiming to some property formerly mortgaged to Edmund Barton, Mary Shakespeare's brother-in-law, joined their son William as a party in the suit.

1592. MARCH 3. Henslowe . . . records that he received £3 16s. 8d. at the first performance of *Harry the Sixth*. The play was repeated on March 7, 11, 16, 28, April 5, 13, 21, May 4, 9, 16, 22, 29, June 12 and 20. For the fifteen performances the gross takings were £32, 8s. 6d. or an average of £2 3s. 3d. a performance. The average for all others plays over the period of three and three-quarter months was £1 14s. 10d.

It seems likely that this is Shakespeare's *I Henry VI*. Nashe in *Piers Penniless His Supplication to the Devil*, entered for publication . . . on August 8, 1592, commented:

> How would it have ioyed brave *Talbot* (the terror of the French) to thinke that after he had lyne two hundred yeares in his Tombe, hee should triumphe againe on the Stage, and have his bones newe embalmed with the teares of ten thousand spectators at least (at severall times) who, in the Tragedian that represents his person, imagine they behold him fresh bleeding?

SEPTEMBER 3. Robert Greene, the pamphleteer, poet, and playwright, died in poverty. . . . Among his papers was a letter addressed "To those Gentlemen his quondam acquaintance, that spend their wits in making plaies," who are usually identified with Marlowe, Nashe, and Lodge. Greene's complaint was that the professional players had battened on the brains of university men like himself, and now they had forseaken him. He continued:

> Base minded men all three of you, if by my miserie you be not warnd: for unto none of you (like mee) sought those burres to cleave: those Puppets (I meane) that spake from our mouths, those Anticks garnisht in our colours. Is it not strange, that I, to whom they all have beene beholding: is it not like that you, to whome they all have beene beholding, shall (were yee in that case as I am, now) bee both at once of them forsaken? Yes trust them not: for there is an upstart Crow, beautified with our feathers, that with his *Tygers hart wrapt in a Players hyde*, supposes he is as well able to bombast out a blanke verse as the best of you: and beeing an absolute *Iohannes fac totum*, is in his owne conceit the onely Shake-scene in a countrey. O that I might intreat your rare wits to be imploied in more profitable courses: & let those Apes imitate your past excellence, and never more acquaint them with your admired inventions.

The phrase "Tygers hart wrapt in a Players hyde" is a parody of a line in *III Henry VI*—"O tiger's heart wrapped in a woman's hide!"—and Greene's passage is a bitter attack on Shakespeare. The letter was printed in Greene's *Groatsworth of Wit*, a short collection consisting of an unfinished novel and other scraps, and put together

Shakespeare for Everyone to Enjoy

for the press by Henry Chettle. It was entered on September 20, 1592. Marlowe had been pointedly referred to in the letter as an atheist and warned to repent in time; he and Shakespeare apparently protested. On December 8, 1592, Chettle's *Kind Heart's Dream* was entered. To this book Chettle added a prefatory epistle in which he wrote:

> With neither of them that take offence was I acquainted, and with one of them I care not if never be: The other, whome at that time I did not so much spare, as since I wish I had, for that as I have moderated the heate of living writers, and might have used my owne discretion (especially in such a case) the Author bee-ing dead, that I did not, I am as sorry as if the originall fault had beene my fault, because selfe have seene his demeanor no lesse civill than be exelent in the qualitie he professes: Besides, divers of worship have reported his uprightness of dealing, which argues his honesty, and his facetious grace in writing that approves his Art.

From these records it seems likely that the Talbot scenes in *I Henry VI* were among the first that Shakespeare wrote. Further, if Shakespeare had been writing plays for some years, Greene could have hardly referred to him as an "upstart," nor could Chettle, in the very small world of the London theater, have pleaded that he had not previously known of him. Shakespeare therefore probably first began to write plays in 1591 or 1592; but some scholars dispute this and claim that he had been actor and playwright since 1587.

1593. APRIL 18. *Venus and Adonis* was entered for publication and was printed with the title page:

VENUS AND ADONIS

*Vilia miretur vulgus: mihi flauus Apollo Pocula Castalia plena ministret aqua.**
*The crowd admirers vile things; for me may yellow-haired Appollo prepare cups full of Castalian water (i.e., from the Muses' spring on Mount Parenassus).

The poem was dedicated

To the Right Honourable Henrie Wriothesley (pronounced and occasionally spelled "Risley"), Earle of Southampton, and Baron of Titchfield.

Right Honourable, I know not how I shall offend in dedicating my unpolisht lines to your Lordship, nor how the worlde will censure mee for choosing so strong a proppe to support to weake a burthen, onelye if your Honour seeme but pleased, I account my selfe highly praised, and vowe to take advantage of all idle hours, till I have honoured you with some graver labour. But if the first heire of my invention prove deformed, I shall be sorie it had so noble a god-father: and never after eare so barren a land, for feare it yeeld me still so bad a harvest. I leave it to your Honourable survey, and your Honor to your hearts content, which I wish may alwaies answere your owne wish, and the worlds hopefull expectation.

Your Honors in all dutie,
WILLIAM SHAKESPEARE.

The Earl of Southampton was at this time nineteen years old. He was regarded as a young man of considerable promise and was conspicuous among the Queen's courtiers for his beauty and intelligence.

Venus and Adonis, though regarded by the sober-minded as an improper poem, established Shakespeare's reputation as a poet. It was reprinted at least nine times during his lifetime.

1594. MAY 9. *The Rape of Lucrece* was entered for printing. This poem too was dedicated

To the Right Honourable, Henry Wriothesley, Earle of Southampton, and Baron of Titchfield.

The love I dedicate to your Lordship is without end: wherof this Pamphlet without beginning is but a superfluous Moity. The warrant I have of your Honourable disposition, not the worth of my untutored Lines makes it assured of acceptance. What I have done is yours, what I have to doe is yours, being part in all I have, devoted yours. Were my worth greater, by duety would shew greater, meane time, as it is, it is bound to your Lordship; To whom I wish long life still lengthened with all happiness.

Your Lordships in all duety,

WILLIAM SHAKESPEARE

From the tone of the dedication it may be inferred that Southampton had shown considerable favor to Shakespeare during the previous twelve months.

1594. DECEMBER 26 AND 27. Payment for performances at Court was made to "William Kempe, William Shakespeare, & Richarde Burbage, servantes to the Lord Chamberleyne." This is the first record which definitely names Shakespeare as a member of the company. Subsequent payments for Court performances were made to John Heminges, who seems to have acted as treasurer for the company.

1596. AUGUST 11. The parish register of the Stratford-on-Avon church records the burial of "Hamnet filius William Shakspere."

OCTOBER 20. William Dethick, Garter Principal King of Arms, granted to John Shakespeare the privilege of bearing a coat of arms, viz.:

Gould, on a Bend Sables, a Speare of the first steeled argent. And for his crest or cognizaunce a falcon his winges displayed Argent standing on a wrethe of his coullers: supporting a Speare Gould steeled as aforesaid sett uppon a helmett with mantelles & tasselles as hath ben accustomed and doth more playnely appeare depicted on this margent: Signefieing hereby & by the authorite of my office aforesaid ratefieing that it shalbe lawfull for the said John Shakespeare gentilman and for his children yssue & posterite (at all tymes and places convenient) to beare and make demonstracon of the same Blazon or Atchevment uppon theyre Shieldes, Targetes, escucheons, Cotes of Arms, pennons, Guydons, Seales, Ringes, edefices, Buyldinges, utensiles, Lyveries, Tombes, or monumentes or otherwise for all lawfull warlyke factes or civile use or exercises, according to the Lawes of Armes, and cust999mes that to gentillmen belongethe without let or interruption of any other person or persons for use or bearing the same.

Thus William Shakespeare in the right of his father was henceforward entitled to call himself "gentleman."

1596. NOVEMBER 29. In the Controlment Rolls of the Queen's Bench in the Public Record Office in London occurs an entry that William Wayte craved sureties of the peace against William Shakespeare, Francis Langley, Dorothy Soer, wife of John

Soer, and Ann Lee for fear of death and so forth. A writ of attachment was issued to the Sheriff of Surrey, returnable on November 29.

This entry was discovered by Dr. Leslie Hotson and published in his *Shakespeare versus Shallow* (1931). Of the persons mentioned, Langley was owner of the Swan play-house, which he had built about two years earlier. Wayte was the stepson of a rascally magistrate named William Gardener. Langley himself had claimed sureties of the peace against Gardener and Wayte less than a month earlier. Dr. Hotson discovered many details about Wayte and Gardener, but was unable to find how Shakespeare came into the business or how he had caused anyone to be in fear of his life.

1597. MAY 4. William Shakespeare purchased from William Underhill a house with two barns and two gardens in Stratford-on-Avon for £60 sterling.

This property, known as New Place, was a large house in the center of Stratford. It was then about a hundred years old, built of brick and timber, and of fair size, with a frontage of sixty feet and a depth of seventy feet. Only the foundations now remain.

AUGUST 29. Andrew Wise entered *Richard II* for publication. It appeared soon afterward with the title *The Tragedie of King Richard the second. As it hath beene pub-likely acted by the right Honourable the Lorde Chamberlaine his Servants.* No author's name was given in the 1597 edition, but the play was twice reprinted in 1598 with the addition of *By William Shake-speare.*

OCTOBER 20. Andrew Wise entered for publication "The tragedie of kinge Richard the Third with the death of the Duke of Clarence," which appeared with the title *The Tragedy of King Richard the Third. Containing, His treacherous Plots against his brother Clarence: the pittiefull murther of his innocent nephewes: his tyrannicall ursur-pation: with the whole course of his detested life, and most deserved death. As it hath been lately acted by the Right honourable the Lord Chamberlaine his servants* (see Pl. 14a). No author's name was given in the 1597 edition, but in a second edition dated 1598 is added *By William Shake-speare.*

NOVEMBER 15. The commissioners appointed to collect the subsidy in the ward of Bishopsgate, London, sent in a list of those who had failed to pay their contribution to the subsidy. Included in the names was "William Shackspere," assessed to pay 5s. on £5. Shakespeare's name reappeared in several later lists, but the tax was appar-ently paid in 1600. These records show that before 1596 Shakespeare had lived in the parish of St. Helen's near Bishopsgate, but afterward went to live on the south side of the Thames.

1598. FEBRUARY 4. Owing to a general shortage of corn due to bad summers, there was considerable hoarding of corn. A survey was made of the corn and malt held by individuals in Stratford-on-Avon. Among them it was found that "Wm. Shackespere" held ten quarters. (1 quarter = 8 bushels. "Corn" here means wheat, rye, and oats.)

FEBRUARY 25. Andrew Wise entered for publication "The historye of Henry the iiii[th] with his battaile of Shrewsburye against Henry Hotspurre of the Northe with the conceipted mirthe of Sir John Ffalstoff," which was published under the title *The History of Henrie the Fourth; With the battell at Shrewsburie, betweene the King and Lord Henry Percy, surnamed Henrie Hotspur of the North. With the humorous conceits of Sir John Falstaffe.* No author's name was given in the edition of 1598, but in the second edition printed in 1599 the words *Newly corrected by W. Shake-speare* were added.

JULY 22. James Roberts entered in the Stationers' Register "a booke of the Marchaunt of Venyce, or otherwise called the Jewe of Venyce, Provided, that yt bee not prynted by the said James Robertes or anye other whatsoever without lycence first had from the Right honorable the lord Chamberlen." This is an example of a "blocking entry" . . . whereby the players arranged with Roberts to enter a play to avoid its publication.

SEPTEMBER 7. *Palladis Tamia: Wit's Treasury* by Francis Meres was entered for publication. This book was a large collection of "similitudes" or parallel passages from a vast number of authors. Meres added "A comparative discourse of our English Poets with the *Greeke, Latine, and Italian Poets.*" Shakespeare was mentioned more frequently than any of the other English writers, as one of eight by whom "the English writers, as one of eight by whom "the English tongue is mightily enriched, and gorgeouslie invested in rare ornaments and resplendent abiliments," as one of six who had raised *monumentum aere perennius,* as one of five who excelled in lyric poetry, as one of thirteen "best for Tragedie," as one of seventeen "best for Commedy." Shakespeare was also picked out for special mention not given to the others:

As the soule of *Euphorbus* was thought to live in *Pythagoras*; so the sweete wittie soule of *Ovid* lives in mellifluous & hony-tongued *Shakespeare,* witnes his *Venus* and *Adonis*; his *Lucrece,* his sugred Sonnets among his private friends, &c.

As *Plautus* and *Seneca* are accounted the best for Comedy and Tragedy among the Latines: so *Shakespeare* among the English is the most excellent in both kinds for the stage; for Comedy, witnes his *Gentlemen of Verona,* his *Errors,* his *Love Labors lost,* his *Love labours wonne,* his *Midsummers night dreame,* & his *Merchant of Venice;* for Tragedy his *Richard the 2. Richard the 3, Henry the 4. King John, Titus Adronicus* and his *Romeo and Juliet.*

As *Epius Stolo* said, that the muses would speake with *Plautus* tongue, if they would speak Latin: so I say that the Muses would speake with *Shakespeares* fine filed phrase, if they would speake English.

Mere's remarks are important; they show that by 1598—even before the greatest tragedies were produced—Shakespeare had already firmly established his reputation; and they give a list of twelve plays already written—a valuable piece of evidence for establishing the dates of some of Shakespeare's plays. *Love's Labor's Won* has apparently been lost, unless it is an earlier title of one of the comedies.

SEPTEMBER 20. The Chamberlain's Men acted Ben Jonson's *Every Man in His Humor.* In the 1616 collection of his plays Jonson added the note:

This Comoedie was first Acted, in the yeere 1598. By the then L. Chamberlayne his Servants. The principall Comoedians were.

Will. Shakespeare.		Ric. Burbadge
Aug. Philips.		Joh. Hemings.
Hen. Condel.		Tho. Pope.
Will. Slye.		Chr. Beeston.
Will. Kempe.		Joh. Duke.

OCTOBER 25. Richard Quiney, a citizen of Stratford, being in London on business, partly private and partly on behalf of the corporation, wrote a letter from the Bell in Carter Lane asking for a loan of £30, addressed "To my Loveinge good ffrend & countreymann Mr. W^m. Shackespere." As the sum of £30 in cash was considerable at this time, the letter shows that Shakespeare was a man of some means.

During this year was printed, but without entry in the Stationers' Register, A *Pleasant Conceited Comedie Called, Loves labors lost. As it was presented before her Hignes this last Christmas. Newly corrected and augmented by W. Shakespere.*

1599. FEBRUARY 21. Documents in a lawsuit dated April 28, 1619, show that a lease of the ground on which the Globe playhouse was being built was agreed between Nicholas Brend on the one part, and on the other Cuthbert Burbadge, Richard Burbadge, William Shakespeare, Augustine Phillipps, Thomas Pope, John Heminges, and William Kempe. The details of the shares of the takings in the playhouse to be received by each are also recorded.

During this year appeared *The Passionate Pilgrime By W. Shakespeare.* The book was published by W. Jaggard and contains twenty poems, two of which are sonnets by Shakespeare and three poems from *Love's Labor's Lost.* The rest of the poems are by different writers. It was an indication of Shakespeare's reputation that a printer should pass off such a volume as entirely his.

1600. AUGUST 23. Andrew Wise and William Aspley entered for publication "Muche a Doo about nothinge" and "the second parte of the history of Kinge Henry the iiiith with the humours of Sir John Falstaff: Wrytten by master Shakespere." This was the first time that Shakespeare's name was entered in the Stationers' Register. The plays appeared with the titles: *Much Adoe about Nothing. As it hath been sundrie times publikely acted by the right honourable, the Lord Chamberlaine his servants. Written by William Shakespere;* and *The Second part of Henrie the fourth, continuing to his death, and coronation of Henrie the fift. With the humours of sir John Falstaffe, and swaggering Pistoll. As it hath been sundrie times publikely acted by the right hounourable, the Lord Chamberlaine, his servants. Written by William Shakespeare.*

OCTOBER 8. Thomas Fisher entered for publication "A booke called A mydsommer nightes Dreame." The play appeared with the title: *A Midsommer nights dreame. As it hath beene sundry times publickely acted, by the Right honourable, the Lord Chamberlaine his servants. Written by William Shakespeare.*

OCTOBER 28. Thomas Hays by consent of James Roberts entered "a booke called the booke of the merchant of Venyce." The play appeared with the title: *The most excellent Historie of the Merchant of Venice. With the extreame cureltie of Shylocke the Jewe towards the sayd Merchant, in cutting a just pound of his flesh; and the obtayning of Portia by the choyse of three chests. As it hath beene divers times acted by the Lord Chamberlaine his Servants. Written by William Shakespeare. . . .*

1601. SEPTEMBER 8. The parish register of the Stratford-on-Avon church records the burial of "Mr. Johannes Shakspere." This was Shakespeare's father.

1602. JANUARY 18. John Busby entered, but immediately assigned to Arthur Johnson, "A booke called An excellent and pleasant conceited commedie of Sir John Faulstof and the merry wyves of Windesor." The quarto which followed is entitled. *'A Most pleasaunt and excellent conceited Comedie, of Syr John Falstaffe, and the merrie*

Wives of Windsor, Entermixed with sundrie variable and pleasing humors, of Syr Hugh the Welch Knight, Justice Shallow, and his wise Cousin M. Slender. With the swaggering vaine of Auncient Pistoll, and Corporall Nym. By William Shakespeare. As it hath bene divers times Acted by the right Honorable my Lord Chamberlaines servants. Both before her Majestie, and else-where.

The text of the play printed in this edition is a garbled and pirated version, very different from the play as known in the first folio.

MAY 1. William Combe and John Combe of Stratford-on-Avon sold to "William Shakespere" one hundred and seven acres of arable land in old Stratford for the sum of £320. The deed was delivered to Gilbert Shakespeare "to the use of the within named William Shakespere." Gilbert was Shakespeare's younger brother, and Shakespeare himself seems to have been in Stratford-on-Avon at the time.

JULY 26. James Roberts entered in the Stationers' Register "A booke called the Revenge of Hamlett Prince Denmarke as yt was latelie Acted by the Lord Chamberleyen his servantes." No edition of 1602 is known. This was apparently another "blocking entry." . . .

SEPTEMBER 28. Walter Getley transferred a cottage in Walkers Street (alias Dead Lane) in Stratford-on-Avon to "William Shackespere."

1603. MAY 19. Queen Elizabeth died on March 24. The new King, James I, took over the Lord Chamberlain's players as the King's Men. A license was accordingly issued to "our Servanutes Lawrence Fletcher, William Shakespeare Richard Burbage, Augustyne Phillippes, John Henninges, Henrie Condell, William Sly, Robert Armyn, Richard Cowly, and the rest of theire Assosiates freely to use and exercise the Arte and faculty of playing Comedies, Tragedies, histories, Enterludes, moralls, pastoralls, Stage plaies and Suche others like as theie have alreadie studied or herafter shall use or studie aswell for the recreation of our lovinge Subjectes as for our Solace and pleasure when wee shall thincke good to see them duringe our pleasure."

Ric. Burbadge.	Will. Shake-Speare.
Aug. Philips.	Joh. Hemings.
Will. Slye.	Hen. Condel.
Joh. Lowin.	Alex. Cooke.

During this year was printed a garbled and pirated version of *Hamlet* entitled: *The Tragicall Historie of Hamlet Prince of Denmarke By William Shake-speare. As it hath beene diverse times acted by his Highnesse servants in the Cittie of London: as also in the two Universities of Cambridge and Oxford, and elsewhere.*

1604. MARCH. King James made a royal progress through the City of London, with his various servants in attendance. The players being Grooms of the Chamber, four yards of red cloth for liveries was given to "William Shakespeare, Augustine Phillips, Lawrence Fletcher, John Hemminges, Richard Burbidge, William Slye, Robert Armyn, Henry Cundell, and Richard Cowley."

During this year was printed a second version of *Hamlet*, entitled: *The Tragicall Historie of Hamlet, Prince of Denmarke. By William Shakespeare. Newly imprinted and enlarged to almost as much againe as it was according to the true and perfect Coppie.* . . . As copies of this version are dated 1604 and 1605, it was probably issued late in 1604.

Shakespeare for Everyone to Enjoy

1605. MAY 4. Augustine Phillips, one of the King's Men, made his will and died shortly afterward, leaving "to my Fellowe William Shakespeare a thirty shillings peece in gould." To other members of the company he also left money, thirty shillings to Henry Condell and Christopher Beeston, and twenty shillings each to Lawrence Fletcher, Robert Armin, Richard Cowley, Alexander Cook, and Nicholas Tooley.

JULY 24. Ralph Huband, in consideration of the sum of £440, assigned to "William Shakespear" a half of all the tithes of Stratford, Old Stratford, Welcombe, and Bushopton, and half the tithes of the parish of "Stratford-upon-Avon." This investment yielded Shakespeare about £60 a year.

1607. JUNE 5. The parish register of the Stratford-on-Avon church records the marriage of "M. John Hall gentleman & Susanna Shaxpere." Susanna was Shakespeare's elder daughter, born in 1583. John Hall was a doctor of medicine well known in the neighborhood.

NOVEMBER 26. Nathaniel Butter and John Busby entered in the Stationers' Register a book called "Master William Shakespeare his historye of Kinge Lear, as yt was played before the Kinges majestie at Whitehall, uppon Sainct Stephens night at Christmas Last [that is, December 26, 1606] by his majesties servantes playinge usually at the Globe on the Banksyde." A quarto was published in 1608.

1608. FEBRUARY 21. The parish register of the Stratford-on-Avon church records the christening of "Elizabeth dawghter to John Hall gentleman." This was Shakespeare's first grandchild.

AUGUST 9. William Ostler, gentleman, of London agreed to rent the Blackfriars playhouse to Richard Burbage, John Hemings, William Shakespeare, Cuthbert Burbage, Henry Condell, and Thomas Evans for a period of twenty-one years.

SEPTEMBER 9. The parish register of the Stratford-on-Avon church records the burial of "Mayry Shaxspere, wydowe." This was Shakespeare's mother.

DECEMBER 17. "William Shackspeare," gentleman, began to take proceedings in the Stratford court against John Addenbrooke, gentleman, to recover a debt of £6. The case went on for some months.

1609. JANUARY 28. Richard Bonion and Henry Walleys entered for publication "a booke called the history of Troylus and Cressida," which appeared under the title: *The Historie of Troylus and Cresseida. As it was acted by the King Majesties servants at the Globe. Written by William Shakespeare.*

A second issue appeared in the same year with the title: *The Famous Historie of Troylus and Cresseid. Excellently expressing the beginning of their loves, with the conceited wooing of Pandarus Prince of Licia. Written by William Shakespeare.*

MAY 20. Thomas Thorpe entered for publication "a Booke called Shakespeares sonnettes," which appeared under the title *"Shakes-speares Sonnets. Never before Imprinted.*

During the year also appeared: *The Late, And much admired Play, Called Pericles, Prince of Tyre. With the true Relation of the whole Historie, adventures, and fortunes of the said Prince: As also, The no lesse strange, and worthy accidents, in the Birth and Life, of his Daughter Mariana. As it hath been divers and sundry times acted by his Majesties Servants, at the Globe on the Banck-side. By William Shakespeare.*

1611. JANUARY. "William Shackspeare" and others started a suit in the Court of

Chancery arising out of the ownership of the tithes which Shakespeare had purchased in 1605.

SEPTEMBER 11. The name of "Mr. William Shackspere" occurs in a list of those contributing toward the prosecuting of a bill in Parliament for the better repair of the highways.

1612. MAY 11. "William Shakespeare" of Stratford-on-Avon in the County of Warwick, gentleman, of the age of forty-eight years or thereabouts, gave evidence in London in the case of *Belott vs. Mountjoy*. The evidence in the case shows that in 1604 Shakespeare was lodging in the house of Christopher Mountjoy, a wigmaker of Huguenot origin, in Cripplegate Ward in the City of London. Shakespeare had helped to negotiate a marriage between Christopher Mountjoy's daughter Mary and Stephen Belott, Mountjoy's apprentice. At the time Mountjoy had promised a dowry, which was not paid. Belott therefore sued his father-in-law, and Shakespeare was summoned as witness to the promises made at the bethrothal. Shakespeare however in his evidence could not remember the details. Shakespeare's signature was appended to his deposition; he signed his name as "Willm. Shakp."

1613. JANUARY 28. John Combe of Stratford left £5 in his will to "Mr. William Shackspere."

MARCH 10. Henry Walker, citizen and minstrel of London, in consideration of the sum of £140 conveyed a dwelling house erected over the great gate of the former Blackfriars Monastery to "William Shakespeare of Stratford Upon Avon in the Countie of Warwick gentleman, William Johnson, citizein and Vintener of London [and host of the Mermaid Tavern], John Jackson, and John Hemmyng of London gentlemen." Shakespeare paid the money; the other three were apparently acting as his trustees. One copy of the agreement, now in the Guildhall, London, bears Shakespeare's signature, in which he spelled his name "William Shakspē."

MARCH 31. The steward of the Earl of Rutland recorded in his accounts the payment "to Mʳ. Shakspeare in gold about my Lorde's impreso. xliiijs; to Richard Burbage for paynting and making yt, in gold xliiijs."

This "impresa" was a symbolic device with appropriate motto borne on the shield of those taking part in a tilt or tournament. These tilts were usually held on the anniversary of the Sovereign's assession (Queen Elizabeth, November 17; King James, March 24). Burbage was well known as a painter as well as an actor.

OCTOBER 28. An agreement was made between "William Shackspeare, of Stretford in the county of Warwicke, gent," and William Replingham of Great Harborough in the County of Warwick that Replingham would recompense Shakespeare for any decrease in his yearly value of tithes which might occur by reason of any enclosure or decay of tillage meant and intended by the said William Replingham. Hereafter Shakespeare's name occurs several times in various Stratford records concerning tithes and enclosures.

1616. FEBRUARY 10. The parish register of the Stratford-on-Avon church recorded the marriage of "M. Tho Queeny tow Judith Shakspere," Shakespeare's younger daughter.

MARCH 25. William Shakespeare made his will. This will was written on three large sheets of parchment, and is now in Somerset House, London. The principal bequests were to his younger daughter Judith, £150, with a futher £150 on trust; to his sister Joan Hart, £20, all wearing apparel, and the use for life of the house which she occupied; £5 to each of his nephews; to Elizabeth Hall, his granddaughter, all his plate except the broad silver-gilt bowl, which went to Judith; money to buy memorial rings to five Stratford friends; 26s. 8d. each to his fellows John Heminges, Richard Burbage, and Henry Condell to buy rings; to his wife his second-best bed, with its furniture; to this daughter Susanna Hall of New Place two houses in Henley Street, and all other lands; and the residue, including all plate and household goods, to Susanna Hall and her husband.

The will was much corrected and revised, and signed at the foot of each of the three pages. Shakespeare's bequest of the second-best bed, and nothing else, to his wife has been much discussed. As widow she was entitled to a third of the income of the estate and to remain in the house. There is therefore no reason to suppose the bequest of the second-best bed, made as an interlinear afterthought, was necessarily a sign either of contempt or of especial affection for the widow.

APRIL 23. The monument in the Stratford church records that Shakespeare died on April 23.

APRIL 25. The register in the Stratford church records the burial of "Will. Shakspere, gent."

Shakespeare was buried within the church in the chancel, and over the grave was laid a stone with the inscription:

GOOD FREND FOR JESUS SAKE FORBEARE,
TO DIGG THE DUST ENCLOASED HEARE!
BLESTE BE Y^E MAN Y^T SPARES THES STONES,
AND CURST BE HE Y^T MOVES MY BONES.

A tablet was erected on the north wall of the chancel which contains a bust within an arch. . . . The inscription reads:

IVDICIO PYLIUM, GENIO SOCRATEM, ARTE MARONEM:
   TERRA TEGIT, POPULUS MÆRET, OLYMPUS HABET.

STAY PASSENGER, WHY GOEST THOU BY SO FAST?
READ IF THOU CANST, WHOM ENVIOUS DEATH HATH PLAST,
WITH IN THIS MONUMENT SHAKSPEARE: WITH WHOME,
QUICK NATURE DIDE: WHOSE NAME DOTH DECK Y^E
   TOMBE,
FAR MORE THEN COST: SIEH ALL, Y^T HE HATH WRITT,
LEAVES LIVING ART, BUT PAGE, TO SERVE HIS WITT.
                              ORITT AÑO DO^I 1616
                        AETATIS - 53 DIE 23 AP².

Shakespeare's Tomb

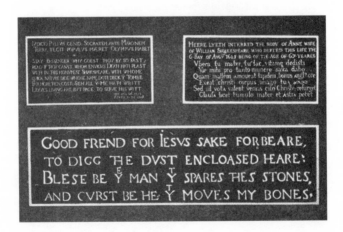

Appendix II

Shakespeare's Will

Vicesimo quinto die [Januarii]* (*The words which have been erased are put between brackets; those which have been interlined are printed in italics.) *Martii*, anno regni domini *nostri* Jacobi, nunc regis Argliæ, &c., decimo quarto, et Scotiæ xlix°, annoque Domini 1616.

—T. Wmi. Shackspeare

In the name of God, Amen! I William Shackspeare, of Stratford upon Avon in the countie of Warr., gent., in perfect health and memorie, God be praysed, doe make and ordayne this my last will and testament in manner and forme followeing, that ys to saye, ffirst, I comend my soule into the handes of God my Creator, hoping and assuredlie beleeving, through thonelie merittes, of Jesus Christe my Saviour, to be made partaker of lyfe everlastinge, and my bodye to the earth whereof yt ys made. Item, I gyve and bequeath unto my [sonne and]* (*Halliwell-Phillippe reads "sonne in L.") daughter Judyth one hundred and fyftie poundes of lawfull English money, to be paied unto her in the manner and forme foloweng, that ys to saye, one hundred poundes *in discharge of her marriage porcion* within one yeare after my deceas, with consideracion after the rate of twoe shillinges in the pound for soe long tyme as the same shalbe unpaied unto her after my deceas, and the fyftie poundes residwe thereof upon her surrendring *of*, or gyving of such sufficient securitie as the over-seers of this my will shall like of, to surrender or graunte all her estate and right that shall discend or come unto her after my deceas, or *that shee* nowe hath, of, in, or to, one copiehold tenemente, with thappurtenaunces, lyeing and being in Stratford on Avon aforesaied in the saied countye of Warr., being parcell or holden of the man-nour of Rowington, unto my daughter Susanna Hall and her heires for ever. Item, I gyveand bequeath unto my saied daughter Judith one hundred and fyftie poundes more, if shee or anie issue of her bodie be lyvinge att thend of three yeares next ensueing the daie of the date of this my will, during which tyme my executours are to paie her consideracion from my deceas according to the rate aforesaied; and if she dye within the saied tearme without issue of her bodye, then my will ys, and I doe gyve and bequeath one hundred poundes thereof to my neece Elizabeth Hall, and the fiftie poundes to be sett fourth by my executours during the lief of my sister Johane Harte, and the use and proffitt thereof cominge shalbe payed to my saied sister Jone, and after her deceas the saied L shall remaine amongst the children of my saied sister, equallie to be divided amongst them; but if my saied daughter Judith be lyving att thend of the saied three yeares, or anie yssue of her bodye, then my will ys, and soe I devise and bequeath the saied hundred and fyftie poundes to be sett out *by my executours and overseers* for the best benefitt of her and her issue, and *the stock* not to be paied unto her soe long as she shalbe marryed and covert baron [by my executours and overseers]; but my will ys, that she shall have the consideracion yearelie paied unto her during her lief, and, after her deceas, the saied stock and consideracion to bee paied to her children, if she have anie, and if not, to her executours or assignes, she lyving the saied terme after my deceas. Provided that yf suche husbond as she shall att thend of the saied three years be marryed unto, or att anie after, doe sufficientlie assure unto her and thissue of her bodie landes awnswereable to the porcion by this my will gyven unto her, and to be adjudged soe by my executours and overseers, then my will ys, that the said cl. shalbe paied to such husbond as shall make such assurance, to his owne use. Item, I gyve and bequeath unto my saied sister Jone xx. and all my wearing apparrell, to be paied and delivered within one yeare after my deceas; and I doe will and devise unto her *the house* with thappurtenaunces in Stratford, wherein she dwelleth, for her naturall lief, under the yearlie rent of xij.*d.* Item, I gyve and bequeath unto her three sonnes, William Harte, . . . Hart, and Michaell Harte, fyve pounds a peece, to be paied within one yeare after my deceas [to be sett out for her within one yeare after my deceas by my executours, with thadvise and directions of my overseers, for her best profitt, untill her mariage, and then the same with the increase thereof to be paied unto her]. Item, I gyve and bequeath unto [her] *the saied Elizabeth Hall,* all my plate, *except my brod silver and gilt bole,* that I now have att the date of this my will. Item, I gyve and bequeath unto the poore of Stratford aforesaied tenn poundes; to Mr. Thomas Combe my sword; to Thomas Russell esquier fyve poundes; and to Frauncis Collins, of the borough of Warr. in the countie of Warr. gentleman, thirteene poundes, sixe shillinges, and eight pence, to be paied within one yeare after my deceas. Item, I gyve and bequeath to [Mr. Richard Tyler thelder] Hamlett Sadler xxvj.*s.* viij.*d.* to buy him a ringe; to *William Raynoldes gent.,* xxvj.*s.* viij.*d.* to buy him a ringe; to my godson William Walker xx*s.* in gold; to Anthonye Nashe gent. xxvj.*s* viij.*d*; and to Mr. John Nashe xxvj.*s.* viij.*d* [in gold]; *and to my fellowes John Hemynges, Richard Burbage, and Henry Cundell, xxvj.*s.* viij.*d.* a peece to buy them ringes.* Item, I gyve, will, bequeath, and devise, unto my daughter Susanna Hall, *for better enabling of her to performe this my will, and towards the performans thereof,* all that capitall messuage or tenemente with thappurtenaunces, *in Stratford aforesaid,* called the New Place, wherein I nowe dwell, and two messuages or tenementes with thappurtenaunces, scituat, lyeing, and being in Henley streete, within the borough of Stratford aforesaied; and all my barnes, stables, orchardes, gardens, landes, tenementes, and hereditamentes, whatsoever, scituat, lyeing, and being, or to be had, receyved, perceyved, or taken, within the townes, hamletes, villages, fieldes, and groundes, of Stratford upon Avon, Oldstratford, Bushopton, and Welcombe, or in anie of them in the saied countie of Warr. And alsoe all that messuage or tenemente with thappurtenaunces, wherein one John Robinson dwelleth, scituat, lyeing and being, in the Blackfriers in London, nere the Wardrobe; and all my other landes, tenementes, and hereditamentes whatsoever. To have and to hold all and singuler the saied premisses, with theire appurtenaunces, unto the saied Susanna Hall, for and during the terme of her naturall lief, and after her deceas, to the first sonne of her bodie lawfullie yssueing, and to the heires males of the bodie of the saied first sonne lawfullie yssueinge; and for defalt of such issue, to the second sonne of her bodie, lawfullie issueing, and [of] to the heires males of the bodie of the saied second sonne lawfullie yssueinge; and for defalt of such heires, to the third sonne of the bodie of the saied Susanna lawfullie yssueing, and of the heires males of the bodie of the saied third sonne lawfullie yssueing; and for defalt of such issue, the same soe to be and remaine to the ffourth [sonne], ffyfth, sixte, and seaventh sonnes of her bodie lawfullie issueing, one after another, and to the heires of the bodies of the saied fourth, fifth, sixte, and seaventh sonnes lawfullie yssueing, in such manner as yt ys before lymitted to be and remaine to the first, second, and third sonns of her bodie, and to theire heires males; and for defalt of such issue, the said premisses to be and remaine to my sayed neece Hall, and the heires males of her bodie lawfullie yssueinge; and for defalt of such issue, to my daughter Judith, and the heires males of her bodie lawfullie issueinge; and for defalt of such issue, to the right heires of me the saied William Shakspeare for ever. *Item, I gyve unto my wief my second best bed with the furniture.* Item, I gyve and bequeath to my saied daughter Judith my broad silver gilt bole. All the rest of my goodes, chattels, leases, plate, jewels, and household stuffe whatsoever, after my dettes and legasies paied, and my funerall expenses dischardged, I give, devise, and bequeath to my sonne in lawe, John Hall gent., and my daughter Susanna, his wief, whom I ordaine and make executours of this my last will and testament. And I doe intreat and appoint *the saied* Thomas Russell esquier and Frauncis Collins gent. to be overseers hereof, and doe revoke all former wills, and publishe this to be my last will and testament. In witness whereof I have hereunto put my [seale] *hand,* the daie and yeare first abovewritten.

By me WILLIAM SHAKSPEARE.

Witnes to the publyshing hereof,
FRA: COLLYNS
JULYUS SHAWE
JOHN ROBINSON
HAMNET SADLER
ROBERT WHATTCOTT

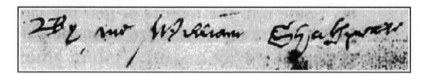

[The original document is preserved in the Principal Probate Registry at Somerset House. Facsimile copy of the original manuscript is available free from The National Archives, www.nationalarchives.gov.uk. This transcription follows E. K. Chambers, *William Shakespeare, a Study of Facts and Problems*, vol. 2. (Oxford: Clarendon Press, 1930), 170–4; a free copy is available at http://ise.uvic.ca/Library/SLT/life/will+1.html.]

Shakespeare in His Study

Appendix III

Bibliography

Bowmer, Angus L., *As I Remember, Adam,* Ashland, Oregon: The Oregon Shakespeare Festival Association, 1975.

Brown, Driver, Briggs, *Hebrew and English Lexicon of the Old Testament,* Lafayette, Indiana, 1981.

Brown, John, B.A., D.D. *The Pilgrim Fathers of New England and Their Puritan Successors,* 1895; *Repub.:* Pasadena, Texas: Pilgrim Publications, 1970.

Chute, Marchette, *Shakespeare of London,* New York: E. P. Dutton, 1949.

Chute, Marchette, *Stories from Shakespeare,* New York: World Publishing Co., 1956.

Epstein, Norrie, *The Friendly Shakespeare,* New York: Penguin, 1993.

Gayley, Charles Mills, *Shakespeare and the Founders of Liberty in America,* New York: MacMillan, 1917.

Gielgud, John, *Acting Shakespeare,* New York: Charles Scribner's Sons, 1991.

Hall, Verna M., compiler, *The Christian History of the Constitution of the United States of America,* Vol. I: *Christian Self-Government,* San Francisco: Foundation for American Christian Education, 1966 & subsequent editions from Chesapeake, VA.

Harrison, G. B., *Introducing Shakespeare,* Baltimore: Penguin, 1971.

Harrison, G. B., ed., *Shakespeare Major Plays and Sonnets,* New York: Harcourt, Brace, 1948.

Horizon Magazine Editors, *Shakespeare's England,* New York: American Heritage, 1964.

Howse, Ernest Marshall, *Spiritual Values in Shakespeare,* New York: Abingdon, 1955.

Hugo, Victor, *William Shakespeare,* London: Hurst and Blackett, 1864.

Leithart, Peter J., *Brightest Heaven of Invention,* Moscow, Idaho: Canon Press, 1996.

Majault, Joseph, ed., *Shakespeare,* Geneva: Minerva, 1969.

Milward, Peter, *Shakespeare's Religious Background,* Chicago: Loyola University Press, 1975.

Nielson, William Allan and Ashley Horace Thorndike, *The Facts about Shakespeare,* New York: MacMillan, 1918.

Oakes, Edward T., "Shakespeare's Millennium," *First Things,* December, 1999.

Pringle, Roger, ed., *The Shakespeare Houses,* Shakespeare Birthplace Trust, Norwich: Jarrold Publishing, 1998.

Rose, James B., *A Guide to American Christian Education for the Home and School: The Principle Approach,* Palo Cedro, CA: American Christian History Institute, 1987.

Slater, Rosalie J., *Teaching and Learning America's Christian History: The Principle Approach®,* San Francisco: Foundation for American Christian Education, 1965 & subsequent editions from Chesapeake, VA.

Webster, Noah, *An American Dictionary of the English Language,* 1828 Facsimile Edition; reprint, San Francisco: Foundation for American Christian Education, 1967 & subsequent editions from Chesapeake, VA.

Appendix IV

NOAH WEBSTER EDUCATIONAL FOUNDATION

The Word of God is a lamp unto the feet of those
who will follow its truths and
a lantern of liberty for any nation that
will follow its principles.
The Bible reveals the source of all true liberty
for the individual and the nation.

WHO WE ARE:

Noah Webster Educational Foundation is dedicated to turning the heart of the nation back to God. First, by sharing the Word of God as the record of personal liberty through Jesus Christ, our commission is to point the individual heart to Jesus. Secondly, by presenting America's Christian history, our goals are to reveal the glory of God, reveal the source and substance of liberty, and restore Christian values and principles essential to liberty. Uniquely, the art of storytelling is used in lectures, seminars, tapes, and written material to achieve stated goals.

WHO WE SERVE:

We seek to serve any organization, family, or individual that desires a Godly perspective of our heritage. Our lectures, seminars, tapes, and books are excellent educational and inspirational tools for church services, Sunday schools, youth groups, Christian school chapels, classrooms, homeschool events, service organizations, banquets, retreats, summer camps, and holiday programs. Both adults and children alike benefit from the vital message of America's Christian heritage.

CURRENTLY:

We have begun writing a series of novels for ages 12 though 15, which we hope will touch the adult market as well with the adventure, mystery, and drama of history. The novels are designed to reveal the miraculous hand of God in the events of men and nations, as well as give the reader a personal encounter with characters that shape the course of nations. Moral values will be a prominent element of the series. In addition, we are in the process of establishing an annual four-day seminar on American history and government in the California gold rush country.

Why We Adopted the Project of Helping to Publish
Shakespeare for Everyone to Enjoy by Rev. David R. Brown

To help preserve our culture:

The plays of William Shakespeare set a standard of excellence for the English language, and establish the author as a consummate authority on human nature. In addition to the use of the language, the characters of William Shakespeare make his plays a timeless and revered part of our culture.

To help ensure that Shakespeare is preserved and produced as the author intended.

Rev. David Brown is a strong advocate for keeping Shakespeare pure. We support Rev. Brown's effort to see the Bard's work preserved for future generations with the author's original intent, and taught for the beauty of the language and the insight into human character.

To help make the work of William Shakespeare enjoyable for every sphere of society.

Pastor Brown wonderfully reaches out to everyone with the intent of breaking down preconceived ideas that prevent people from appreciating the mastery, mystery, and majesty of the greatest playwright of all times.

To support a man of great character and purpose.

Some say we have few real heroes today, but Rev. David Brown is a hero. Unafraid to stand for his principles and never faltering to accomplish his goals, Rev. David Brown is a man of great character.

For all of these reasons it has been our privilege to help to publish *Shakespeare for Everyone to Enjoy* as a project of The Noah Webster Educational Foundation.   —Belinda Beth Ballenger

Appendix V

The Foundation for American Christian Education &

The Principle Approach® to Learning

America's Christian History, Education, & Government

$\mathcal{A}$merica's liberty and the self-governing nature of her citizens are indissolubly linked—it is the character of each individual American that enables America to be free. This is the key truth that compelled our founders, Miss Verna Hall and Miss Rosalie Slater, to establish the Foundation for American Christian Education in 1965 to publish and teach America's Christian history.

The Foundation for American Christian Education (FACE) traces its origins and mission to Verna Hall, a historian who rediscovered in the 1950s the long-forgotten treasure of America's Christian history by reading for herself the primary source documents that led to the establishment of the United States. For the first time, she saw the founders' Godly vision for our nation, and her findings inspired her to remind Americans of the call and blessing of God on America. With this purpose in mind, she compiled historical documents recording America's Christian history into a book, *The Christian History of the Constitution of the United States of America*, Vol. I: *Christian Self-Government* (CHOC I).

In 1965, Miss Hall was joined in her work by Rosalie Slater, a gifted teacher and scholar inspired by CHOC I, who believed that the hope of the United States lay in teaching America's true history to children. She believed that equipping the next generation, one child at a time, with the principles and Christian character necessary for clear thinking and self-government was the only enduring way to restore our national character and its natural consequence, liberty. Miss Slater therefore developed a program for teaching CHOC I to children of all ages, drawing out seven key principles from Miss Hall's text: Miss Hall and Miss Slater established the Foundation in order to publish the program in *Teaching and Learning America's Christian History: The Principle Approach®*. In the course of her research, Miss Slater rediscovered the original method of American education (the Principle Approach®) that produced the true scholars of our founding generation, who were equipped with a Biblical worldview and personal integrity. Together, Miss Hall and Miss Slater mentored many citizens, parents, and educators in America's true heritage and trained them to teach it to others using this proven method. The fruit of the Foundation's work is evident in the many ministries, organizations, and schools formed in response to their efforts to preserve and teach America's Christian history and method of early American education. They longed to restore to every American child his birthright—the truth of his Christian heritage.

The Principle Approach® has been called "reflective teaching and learning." It is America's historic method of Biblical reasoning which places the Truths (or principles) of God's Word at the heart of education. Each subject is predicated upon God's Biblical principles and students are taught to think and reason from principles and leading ideas, using the notebook method to research, reason, relate, and record (also called the 4-Rs).

FACE has developed a K–12 curriculum for teaching with the Principle Approach®. Called *The Noah Plan*®, it treasures and develops the individuality of each student while teaching him to reason using Biblical principles. Every subject in *The Noah Plan*® is presented in its context—as the gift of God for His glory and our blessing—and builds a solidly Biblical worldview in students. Principle Approach® students achieve academic excellence and are well-equipped to protect America's liberty, understanding the Biblical principles upon which our freedoms and government are based.

THE FOUNDATION FOR AMERICAN CHRISTIAN EDUCATION is headquartered in Chesapeake, Virginia. For more information about FACE, the Principle Approach®, and *The Noah Plan*®, we invite you to visit our Web site, www.face. net or contact us at:

The Foundation for American Christian Education
P.O. Box 9588, Chesapeake, Virginia 23321-9588
800-352-3223 • info@face.net

About the Author

David R. Brown began acting as the lead in his sixth grade class play. In junior high he assisted the teacher in directing by overseeing the stage hands and coaching students' acting. In high school, he first performed readings from Shakespeare. In college he directed a pageant so successful it was repeated with three other groups. His greatest role was the lead in the play *J. B.* by Archibald McLeish, a modern setting for the book of *Job*. David Brown has many years of experience in education. He was the founder and superintendent for eleven years of Christian Heritage Academy, Fremont, California, a K–12 private school. He has lectured on Shakespeare at Ashland, Oregon every summer since 1969, and has directed young people in performances of three of Shakespeare's plays. David Brown is Pastor of New Life Presbyterian Church, Castro Valley, California, and his biography appears in *Who's Who in American Education, Who's Who in America,* and *Who's Who in the World.*

For information about this book or
to contact the author for interviews,
reviews, & public appearances, go to:

HELEN COOK

800-792-1512 • 979-922-1512

Helen.Cook@PrimeStarPublicity.com

www.PrimeStarPublicity.com

For Book Sales:
contact the publisher.